A
year in the making

This anthology of poetry was one year in the making. Beginning in July 2021 and running to July 2022 I wrote or reimagined more than 300 poems. There are many new poems and some old re-writes from when I began writing poetry.

The book is broken into months and shows a journey through my mind as each month came and went, with nature often being a common factor.

I need to thank a few people that helped make this body of work possible. My kids will always be top of the list as they are my constant inspiration.

Next up is a fellow poet on All Poetry, Kaye has helped push me to write at least one poem every day during America's National Poetry Month which often turned into many more. Thanks, can never really convey what this level of writing achieved and the changes in me personally.

Cheers Kaye my dear friend this one is for you also.

JULY 2021

Black Ice
On the surface you lie,
waiting, unseen, a predator.
Chameleon shades mask
an accident waiting to happen.

Broken
Burned.
Searing heat from painted lips,
engulfed his mind, memory stripped.

All of him she stole away,
till one morn she went her way.
A hollow mattress and plastic daisies,
dark reminders for the crazy.

Click
Watching. Waiting.
The perfect shot,
he knows it, feels it,
almost tastes it.

Scanning
back and forth,
loading their images into his mind,
seeking her, knowing she will bring perfection.
Whirring whispers bring focus,
he smiles.
Click.

Countdown
Neon digits reflect death,
illuminating beads of sweat
coursing like angry rivers from his brow.

Pliers of life hover,
red or black, choices,
a simple snip
before the countdown falls.

Dance of the scents
A lilac duvet offers a peek,
a brief opening to your centre.
Sweet aromatic need cascades forth,
riding rampant winds seeking a mate.

Following the passage of the sun,
time deserts them,
each petal offers chastity,
entrance denied beneath a birthing moon.

Dawn arrives,
pale lavender blankets awaken,
drawing back neath sensual dewdrop touches
alive, waiting,
for the dance of the scents.

Elemental Battle
Ripped from slumber
she awaits the onrushing evil.
Bathed in dark clouds,
he comes, master of the storm.

Horizons lost,
tentacles of bark at the ready,
Mother Nature waits.

Drinking tea with the devil
I knew my time was up.
Contract foreclosed, final moments upon me,
an outcome written in blood
and concreted when last we met.

Thunderous hooves herald your arrival,
opening the door, I beckon you inside.

Cuppa's in hand, we talk of this and that,
intellectual nothings till the steam falls,
like two old chums reunited for a moment.

Body slumping, tea finished,
my final thought is a laugh,
wow, the devil drinks Earl Grey.

Home is subjective
Home.
How I longed for fond memories,
a childhood of innocence and joy.

GUESS NOT!

Home.
Moments of quiet,
broken only by the soft scratch of pen on paper.
Words flow in chaotic cohesion,
building into coherent thoughts of emotions and desires.

This is home,
this is where the smiles are real,
a place filled with musings and writings of **US**.

Hiding my monster
Smiles,
broken and genuine,
drift across uncertain lips.
Kind words flow like bandages,
easing your pain and hiding mine.

Anxiety,
my twin, my monster,
briefly buried behind broken smiles.

Ragged breath capitulates toward 5 pm,
trying not to run a given.

Lake
Fathomless.
Erie in silence, beautiful in serenity.
Unchanged as seasons falter,
sincere in your beauty.

One hell of a day
They lined up before her,
echoes of humanity,
transformed into their true nature,
salivating for a drop of angel blood.

The gates slam shut,
sword in hand she steps forward,
en masse they rush.
The first one falls, she dons a smile,
this is going to be one hell of a day.

Rock Pool 1
They had been here before.
The inhabitants of Rock Pool 1,
held in limbo by the mercy of the tides.

A grain of sand at a time they begin,
remnants of their lives cast to the debris fields,
then lost in shadow, as the sun slips behind the clouds.

Sullied
Quill in hand he hesitates.
Each imperfection, every broken thought,
mere sullied paper scraps carpeting his future.

Alone with his failures,
he stares,losing himself
in the tainted paper virgin before him,
tears mercifully clouding his vision.

Taking secrets to the grave
Pristine and finely cut,
lawns like Wimbledon
a fitting backdrop for marble italics.

Kneeling by your side,
my heart pours forth my life, loves and secrets.
Silence greets my meanderings,
a warmth spreads and my smile flitters briefly.
Taking a secret to the grave,
finally makes a little more sense.

Sun-kissed
The youthfulness she had once enjoyed,
lost in each arid line
tearing across her ageing face.

Memories of hot summers
course through her parched skin
masking the moisture-less tears she cries.

Bronzed under merciless suns,
a tanned waxen countenance stares back
finally, she understands her mistake.

Heatwave
No air,
each breath laced in fire,
dry and burnt, ragged lungs fight to survive.
Water oozes from porous skin in rivulets,
a salty meal for industrious insects
ready to face death for a feed.

Each surface born in hell,
seared fingerprints, a small reminder of man's existence.
Heat shimmering in rolling heat,
fanning the melting pot of summer.

Closing my childhood
Digital death came for you.
The non-paper brigade
counts time on your life.
Goodbye to the book,
my old friend.

Silent Scribbles
Broken pens pour forth nothing.
Silent scribbles,
festering like lies sullying virgin sheets,
waiting till the new gobbles up the old.

Poetic mercy, once his saviour,
offers hope over mutilated thoughts,
challenging the silence, daring the impossible,
offering light in the dark.

In the blink of an eye
Beneath dark lashes,
crystal blue optics stir the blood,
riveting my gaze to yours,
seeking entrance to the darkest depths of my soul.
Petals unfurled inwards at your passing,
even the flowers gave up the ghost,
offering pale reminders of life within the blink of an eye.

Hiding out
Stench, strong and vile,
I hide among the putrid rot of man.

One mistake.

A slip of a blade,
an innocent fell.

The chase began,
in a spilled inkwell,
darkness saved me.

August 2021

Little Lies
little lies
hints of soot
bigger lies feed disgust
life's canvas sullied dark
creativity, losing spark
poetry sighs
goodbye

After the owl and the pussycat
it began as a tale in a boat
lost at sea, still afloat
a dream was born in a starry night
if I survived and earned the right

to look upon your feline face
one more chance I hoped to take
a port appeared in twinkling lights
hope repaid for man and wife

away from the ocean I shall stay
living on land holding sway
death cheated on a calming sea
baring hope from you to me

into your arms I duly fall
thanking the heavens for hearing my call
in a boat I uttered a wish
ending that tale with our kiss

Life is precious anywhere
sidewalk
broken hope
offers a shoot
fighting for life
again

Doggy morns
pensive saliva-tinted greetings
awaken the morn
back turned
bed gone
sleep yours

Love's ballad
angel choruses, a lyrical throng
heartfelt ballads, embracing song

perfect music brought to the fore
born of love forevermore

Summer lullabies
breezes rise
gentle caresses
awaken stirring leaves
whispered lullabies capturing summer

songs
for the drowsy mind
awoken in colour explosions

Selective sensory avoidance
civility and kindness
priceless
fee free
except
a heart and a little time
selective sensory avoidance
the curse of many
fixed by few

Doors
heart lurching
whispers echoed
doors close, doors open
they had no idea

rattling doorframes
they will learn
chances are hers alone
and she'll take them

Morning song
lilting avian melodies
caress the senses
light arias
awaken the dawn
in feathered classical chorus

Cloud-sculpting
cloud watching
a study in pictures
I see them all
endless galleries of masterpieces
crafted in shades of blue and white

Facing her demon
falling into herself
memories catch on past indiscretions

poisonous choice holds the backdrop
enigmatic smiles slaying her demon

Despondent
lethargic deduction
places pen on paper
oppressive silence
kills the mood in amplified despondency.

Wisteria Jack (Wisteria Acrostic)
wildness unchecked, savage
iridescent violet explosions
spray empurpled fragments
trailing lavender rockets in a cobalt sky
enigmatic floral tapestries
ripple across broken trestles
invading the heavens
attracting Jack to a new beanstalk

Goodbye we missed
death ripped you from my side
unbidden, convicting my heart to solitary

kneeling by your side
cold earth saturates feeling
consigning your former warmth to memory
tears feeding pallid flowers of rememberance

soft wings alight
butterfly counsel callled
listening to confessional tones of pain
breathless, tears shed, quiet returned
my confidant rises, caught on your breeze

The final storm
Thunderdome.
Storm clouds
swelling rage, building fury,
whipped into frenzied anger.
Cradling the panicked world,
storms rifle souls
body counts rise,
armageddon.

September 2021

Happy now
look deeply
don't YOU dare look away
see the child I was
when we met

look up
see what you left behind
nothing

Summer's transformation
summer leaves transform
cocktails of beauty and death
serenely drifting
alighting upon their birthplace
trodden underfoot in nature's cemetery

Summer's end
temperatures slipped
single digits holding sway
clawing, clinging to life

summer's end?
perhaps

Waiting for the bird
Clock face forgotten, she waits,
twin doors engulf her vision.
Heart quickening, she almost feels it.
Cuckoo!
Head rocking backwards, a small giggle escapes,
59 minutes begin their slow count.
Eyes fixated on the doors; the game begins again.

Kiss of an Autumn morn
toes peeking
bitten
neath' mercury slides

heat hazes of bought warmth
fog windows
outer meeting inner

September chilly morns
kiss season's change
falling again into Autumn

Petaled tears
Upon a stalk, a flower bloomed,
late in season, quickly doomed.
Lightning winds scathe the land,
offering petaled tears like grains of sand.

When he saw her
Breathless, he watched from afar,
lost in the sunlight playing through her hair.
First smile offered,
his heart dared to tear from his chest.
Mind swirling, senses adrift,
he reaches for her hand.

Private fools
If privacy is your goal,
earless rooms for your dark business depravities,
capital letters emblazoning your intentions,
a mistake.

Black on white or reversed,
gold to catch all light,
draws moths to keyholes
and your secrets are hidden no more.

The mystery of the bikini
Watching TV the other night,
I beheld a comic sight.
A girl did quickly towel grab,
to hide her smalls, I know quite drab.

A night slid by, dawn arose,
camera pans to a beached cove.
Lo and behold, our girl stands fair,
body uncovered with little care.

From these events, I drew a simple view,
a bikini is really nothing new.
Just a bra and knicker set for the public eye,
that costs a fortune, I wonder why?

Agoraphobic pandemic
Law directs every move,
closing doors, taking friends.
The new norm brings shopping to the door,
safe, brief, exposure, from step to cupboard.
Sunlight I once cherished,
now plagues my hooded vision in tiny glimpses.
I stare through rain-streaked glass bars,
safely hidden in a 14x12 prison cell.

After the music died
I lay my head,
hiding one ear from death.
Pitiful notes wail, drawing my teeth together,
holding the braying beasts at bay.
Questions echo resentment,
did you listen? take heed of your wife?
and get the bloody thing tuned,
Nope.

Shadow of the kestrel
I sit mesmerised,
your persistence, elegance and skill are a masterpiece.
A dark unmoving shadow,
naked on the grey visage of the world.
Hovering for an eternity,
the starvation of winter lies upon you.

Fervent stealthy movement captures your attention,
a meal for the starving, its own hunger betraying it.
The mildness of winter your ally,
their hibernation lost; eternal sleep their reward.

The arc of the hunter begins,
talons rigid, arrow-straight you descend.
The leaden backdrop can't hide your shadow,
blood turned to ice; fear holds your prey rigid.

For a brief moment,
it will understand the circle of life,
then the cries will end and death will call.
Pangs of hunger briefly sated,
you rise again, a wisp of smoke in a darkening sky.

Fields of gold
Buttercups, dandelions, hold the hue,
summer haze, beauty true.
From top to bottom a field of gold,
emerald stems standing bold.
Yellow heads sway on a summer breeze,
birds for ships skim a golden sea.

A battle of wings, large and small,
Swallows, beetles, heed the call.
Circles of life in a field of gold,
beauty and death, a sight to behold.

Playing with a broken deck
Together we caught wishes in jars,
carving out our life of happiness,
then the pasteboards invaded my dreams.
In an old back room,
dust motes flutter in free neon.
The same bedraggled faces wait,
angry, belligerent, shadows of men.
Eyes smarting from cancerous breaths,
gnarled fingers flick cards across a green ocean,
chip boats bobbing in earnest.

A pause,
nicotine digits caressing a final drag,
stub out life in a flowerpot long devoid of flowers.
Idle fingernails trace a former victim,
hopes reduced to initials, sighing, I wait to add my own.
360 minutes come and gone, is this the one, my shot?
A fabled card, an ace wearing a heart,
unable to make an appearance, lost outside a broken deck.

Cherry Jam
Alive, vibrant, awaiting your gentle touch,
a bath, a long soak,
preambles to the soft duvet of your cuddles.

We were blind, trustful,
the first cut tears out our hearts,
opening a vast conveyor belt of murder.

However.
Did a pit slip by? Are you sure?
Enjoy your jam.

<u>Dance of the seasons</u>

Autumn came early,
her late summer soiree,
burdened beneath cancerous leaves.

Her pointe, practiced and polished,
sinking slowly, untested.
Arms raised in defiance, she leaps,
pirouetting to the mournful aria of fall.

Frenzied platforms wither, unable to capture her,
through lightness of foot she begins her final stand.
Oh! summer faerie, your light begins to dim,
drawing forward the final dance of summer's hope.

<u>His last post</u>
Grizzled but proud.
He had circled the world,
fought across war-torn continents,
offering his heart for queen and country.

His last day of mosquitoes, sand and storms,
endured.

Fatigue bites at muscle and bone,
withering the vibrancy he once wore as a crown.
Staccato drum rolls pepper the hillside,
and somewhere close The Last Post echoes.

<u>Awakening the stars</u>
Prick,
explosions erupt in his mind,
washing sight in neon rainbows.

Night falls, the mind sleeps.
Hunger awakens the fiery breath of need,
pinholed flesh beckons to the stars again.

The edge of night

Pale slivers of light tint the edge of her vision,
adding some relief to the darkness trying to engulf her,
hands grasping the air she seeks solidity.
Fingers drifting through midnight she senses shadows reforming,
disturbed by her passing, ebony to black in fluid movement they dance.
Tentatively she traces her own countenance,
all appears normal, her eyes sit open,
questions form in her mind.
Why is she in perpetual darkness?
Smoky apparitions in shades of onyx swim through her darkened vision,
gone forever are the images to match the sound.
Panic rising she remains lost in a nightmare of jade vistas,
eyes scrabbling she seeks the edge of the night before her,
the twin slivers of light she glimpsed, remaining just out of reach.
Hearts slamming in her chest, the last remnants of sleep slip their guise,
understanding seeks an audience in her mind.
Calming herself, answers begin to form as memory surfaces,
the edge of darkness is eternally hers,
as is the darkened vision of the blind.

Phantom Breaths

Through smoky wraiths of shadow,
I watch and wait.
Nerve endings twitching under sensual touches,
eyes flickering acceptance she drifts into ecstasy.
Molten vapours pour mouth to mouth,
twisted torrid dreams only the beginning of her torment.
I breathe deeply, feeding on the excitement gnawing through her soul,
revelling in the heat oozing from every pore.
Exhale to inhale, life to death,
just another feed for a succubus.

Coffee Black

It began with a single drop,
A tiny prism of colour erupts from the first spatter,
caught in the dying colours of sunset,
they twinkle, a final grasp for life.

Under the deluge,
vale and tree are washed clean of the days grime,
so begins the spring clean.

Darkness falls hiding sight,
but my ears still catch the distant beat.
Gurgling whispers drift from struggling plastic pipes,
a water concerto to bring forth the night.

Listening to the rain

It began with a single drop,
A tiny prism of colour erupts from the first spatter,
caught in the dying colours of sunset,
they twinkle, a final grasp for life.

Under the deluge,
vale and tree are washed clean of the day's grime,
so begins the spring clean.

Darkness falls hiding sight,
but my ears still catch the distant beat.
Gurgling whispers drift from struggling plastic pipes,
a water concerto to bring forth the night.

Flicker
Shadows linger,
mesmerised,
caught in light's web.

Flicker.

Surging, they breach,
the battle was swift,
shadowlands their new home.

Flicker.

Genocide.
Final screams echo,
the death of night has begun.

Broken shells of the past

Using words for nails,
hammer blows fall,
your payback for the hopeful.

Broken shells carpet your past,
a life littered with the forgotten,
a final nail for the present,
goodbye.

Scars
Puckered skin in pearl white,
trails of tiredness or madness,
true testament to the failings of man.

The searing pain long since departed,
yet,
each blemish a harsh reminder of a slip.

A roller coaster ride through emotions,
each failing catalogued, each loss
interpreted by the birth of a new scar.

An open void, a steadily weeping fissure,
wounds of the heart and mind, never to heal.

Escape
Her pain stopped at the door,
mind freed from your forest of pitch.

One step was all it took,
faith carried the second,
freedom the third.

Eyes unshackled,
the morning bows,
multiple suns lift
matching your smile.

Recollection rises,
a snippet of the past offers hope.
Tentatively you grasp at the thought,
relief courses through understanding
the sun still shines in a darkened wood.

No time for bed
Tired and weary, head at a slant,
eyes closing rapidly, sleep perchance.
Adrenalin rush, awake with a start,
minutes lost or did an hour depart.

Bewilderment joins; strange surroundings too,
clarity lost in a house that's new.
Senses creeping reality returned,
hopes of sleep crashed and burned.

Onwards I go into a frenzy of clean,
prices of wipes becoming obscene.
Evening to night, time travelled forward,
tired and weary dreams carry me onward.

Onward to slumber and a restful night,
maybe to dreams or a nightmarish sight.
Calling to me under sandman's song,
exhaustion rode in, sleep forgotten too long.

A passable entry for a home I see,
dotted with character of gifts for free.
Creativity we brought to our home in May,
sleep came a calling and stayed for a day.

The year of the tree
Winter's putrid scent washes over the weary.
Hope rises on lilac winds.
battling with aromatic apple,
the fragrance wars begin for Spring's crown.

Storm clouds howl, creaking fingers lift,
funnelling life into baby buds.
Leaves erupt, soft murmurs betray their presence,
swirling life under a beating sun.

Lips gently brushing willing flesh,
warm air raises hairs upon a willing throat.
Unyielding bark stencils passion upon my back,
oblivious pain beneath my lover's embrace.

Eyes wide open, I lose myself,
the magnificence of nature, breathtaking.
Leaves knitted together offer a canopy of privacy,
for love's awakening amid beauty's forest.

The change was swift,
burnt promises dry my mouth in soot.
The leaves fell, carried to their own demise,
offering the taste of death that carried your goodbye.

Desert flower
Dutifully chase, her final crime,
divorce perchance, but not the time.
Death he wanted, a quick farewell,
so down they rode into hell.

In sands of death, her fingers grasp,
for life, then vengeance, his death perhaps.
Dragging hope with all her power,
help arrived in a desert flower.

Reflections lost in a storm
Night within day on ebony wings glide,
whipping the clouds of war into a frenzy.
Like sailors of old; the flagships ride the squall,
elemental ports open, preparing for war.
Shuffling forward with non-languid grace,
I rest my head upon the cold, ghostly, reflection of you.
Siamese twins; locked together in our transparent mirror,
behind/in front of a prison without bars.

Tinged in black ink; tainted clouds lie in wait, ready
to unleash destruction on an unsuspecting land.
Looking upon your worried face; I grimace,
as each staccato raindrop erupts on the glass.
Hands meeting under crackling thunder, our fingers
trace trails of condensation betraying the fleeting life of the raindrop.
Brothers and sisters, mothers and fathers,
all flowing together into a rivulet of death.

Lifting a finger in absent attention,
I feel for the tears erasing you from existence,
but these tears are yours alone.
My finger scrapes heavily on the aridness of age.
Watery scars now criss-cross your face.
Our time is short, but a fleeting moment in life,
I step back; your mimicked movement,
almost laughing at my unease.

Murky reflections of ill-defined images,
what was once me is now you;
a macabre mime,
being washed from existence.
I see your pain but feel nothing.
Snapping the blinds closed on your rage;
I still feel your anger behind your latted lids,
waiting for the ultimate act of betrayal.

Heavy blue shroud in my grip
I draw our final act to a close,
releasing you to your watery grave.
Reborn in the sunshine, I await your return,
my reflection, no longer lost in the storm.

Thank you my love
The wall around my heart shattered,
when our friendship turned to lust.

In ugly astonishment, I sat
staring at you and him,
failing to see what everyone else did,
a couple brought together by the heavens.

The gods had mocked me again.
Was my emotional torment
their comedy hour.

Needing no encouragement in breathless passion,
you whispered your love on our last night.
I stepped away from the mirror for you,
all my emotions held in reflection.

My skewered heart began beating again.
The sorrow it had suffered briefly forgotten,
coaxed to life under your gentle love-filled utterances.

The wall is impenetrable now, the mirror repaired,
everything flushed away in the outhouse of dejection.

Thank you, my love.

The love token of a rose
On bended knee, I offer this rose to thee,
with love, my heart and all that I be.
I kneel before you in virginal white,
rose upheld, capturing light,
born of love, understanding and truth,
blessed by the gods, not just for youth.

Will you accept my rose as a token of love?
Joining our hearts below and above,
giving life to love born for two,
begun with a white rose, from me to you.

The Pendant
A simple clasp
hides her love.
Silver filigree,
stark against her fallen pose.

Soft bells chime,
avarice glints, pennies clink.
Pendant and past, lost.
A poor price for life.

Moonlight Serenade
midnight falls
baying laughter ripples
lunar predators ride the breeze

moonlit, fur tinged blue
loping
across land, river
pursuing
hunting
a wraith seeking prey

The Last Flowers
lonely stalks
ride autumn's seas
petals nor leaves
no longer seen

neighbours gone
returned to the ground,
whisked away with nary a sound.

October 2021

<u>Enduring isn't closure</u>

I endured.
Moving sideways, never forwards,
I sensed the ripples of change,
a steadily rising eddy trying to engulf me,
overwhelm me, drag me down.

I struggled, I thrashed,
fighting against the onslaught of change.
Fear ruled my every stroke,
understanding slow to materialise
I was scared.
Ultimately I floundered,
ripped from the protective home of my own cocoon.

Rising,
lifted from the broken rocks of the past,
questions searing my mind.

Is this where I belong?
alone in this brave new world.

Does my life still belong to me?
or is my soul forever lost.

I often pondered these thoughts,
never really seeking an answer,
happy in the safety of pondering.
Yes I know, a pale attempt at life.
Fear always crushed the revolt
so I wore a well-worn disguise
and adorned it with a smile.

Still, it saddens me.
The problem stood in stark reality,
questions held no answers, no closure was found,
all because I never said goodbye,
forgot to close the gaping wound
of our past.

Changing

frigid blasts greet the morn
dusting all with icy scorn
aching snowflakes masking pain
dark to white minus rain.

Twins

twins
dark and light
hunting
cat and mouse games begin

Outside my window is a memory

For weeks I watched,
cobblestones lifted then discarded like my youth.
Long gleaming poles take root,
uncaring emblems of modernisation.
Dusk settles and pitch bathes my window,
night after night beneath another council failure.

War or peace? (Is the choice ours?)

Is one dependent on the other?
Can peace truly flourish if the fear of war is the only deterrent?

Strangled beliefs born of fear agitate into inertia,
till all answers are lost to the void.
Two sides, one coin emerges,
twins of light and dark, locked in eternal combat.
Hope abandoned, hope embraced,
each feeding the ravenous needs of the other,
with desolate devastation the ultimate outcome for all.

The moment you cried

Tear streaked mascara,
signs of your internal turmoil.
Hasty breaths, exhale,
your mask returned, beneath a shaky smile.

The fall of Autumn

green bleeds red
amber pales yellow
fading shadows of life
flatlined in cancerous brown
sparse reminders of autumn

autumn's swan song
silenced

Moonlight Serenade (Long version)
Baying laughter ripples as midnight falls,
your presence briefly betrayed to your prey.

Bathed in moonlight, fur tinged in blue,
you lope across your land, seeking, hunting,
memories of your last meal, faintly alive
in the crimson tinged saliva erupting from an eager mouth.

A moment of stealth,
each silent footfall draws you close,
nostrils quivering you scent your meal,
15 becomes 10 becomes 5.
Head lifting, your prey belatedly senses your presence,
but it’s all a little too late.

A moonlight serenade echoes a warning to all,
teeth sink deep, blood flies across gentle breezes of night,
a dance of death begins and the laughter begins anew.

Riverwalk
Time frozen form last we met,
footsteps once carved in mud,
eradicated by half a century.

I marvel at the fury of flood season,
becalmed by your summer babblings,
till awakening beneath each new floral explosion,
littered across your banks.

Wrapped in Autumn

neath' umbrella skies
fading temperatures speak of winter

wrapped together in autumn
our golden season
scatters life for our pleasure

Autumn's end

pallid rays
disrobe skeletal wraiths
breeze caught
final pirouettes
dance across littered sidewalks
lamenting season change

Intertwined
Intertwined,
two hearts in unison
caught in the staccato beat of youth

for me a commitment,
for you just carved hearts on a tree

Sea Star
lying in majesty
five points carve out her home

catching eddies
spinning intentionless
pastures new beckon

leaving the old to her children
riding moonbeams of time
briefly kissing her cousins of the sky
she awaits the mercy of the tides.

Death of a friendship in a single night
Inseparable we began,
children to gawky teens we travelled together.
The stolen kisses of infancy, remembered fondly,
till a friendship died in staccato heartbeats of drunken lust.

Music of the Rain
Thunderous echoes release the storm.
Beneath the deluge,
gurgling waters traverse honeycombs of guttering,
seeking to reunite with their other fallen brethren.

Tear streaked windows obscure my view,
closing my eyes, I listen.
Soft murmurs caress my senses
unfurling the rain’s concerto to me.

Cymbals crash, moving horizons,
a heartbeat later, the final drops fall into a muted silence.

You made me this way
blow after blow,
sanity recoiling
seeking a haven
but payback is coming

Twisted Fairytale
Born of wealth I would want for nothing.
Christening day duly arrived,
out came the glad rags and painted smiles,
mere lies for the camera.

Fairy grandmothers were ushered in amid much fanfare,
bestowing their doctrines,
upon the forehead soaked angel before them.

Silence falls,
the matriarch waits for no-one,
shuffling forward on broken crutches,
she seeks an audience of one.

Two score plus one from this day,
you will befall an accident,
I offer a playful smile and a tug on the hairs of her mole.

20.5 years pass in sheer boredom,
lessons on ladylike endeavours,
very quickly meet an eye roll, stamp of foot
or any other act of petulance or disdain I can muster.

Turning a corner, I watch Cupid's arrow arc by my head,
striking firmly into a member of the visiting dignitary, Thomas.
I wait for my own arrow to find me,
much like the Borg from my youth, RESISTANCE IS FUTILE.
Opening my heart I wait and he misses,
straight between the eyes,
love versus logic, love loses this time.

I feel the wave start at my feet, tearing swiftly forward,
Mama is first, eyes closing a soft snuffle escapes,
then she is falling with all the grace of a corpse.
Papa follows suit, till 1 by 1 they all fall,
The world sleeps around me,
dreaming the dreams of eternity.

AN ACCIDENT, she had said,
just a little bit of an extreme Grams to stop me having sex.

The limitless beauty of imagination
Born in a moment, an idea birthed,
bare-bones, building blocks of hope.

Thought traversed its limits,
infusion a sentence away,
beauty exploding upon the page.

Limitless,
feelings - colours - emotions - pour forth,
crafting a hopeful masterpiece of poetic beauty.

Music of the morn
From black to grey,
night furls its ebony wings.
The first chorus of the morn,
carries a lilt to a waking world.

First rays peep above the horizon,
different warbles join the throng,
singing with gusto, welcoming life,
offering a lament to the passing of night.

Sunrise passes,
the morning chorus crescendos,
falling swiftly beneath the wail of hungry mouths.

Painting her world
A gift from father to daughter,
monochrome landscapes await her touch,
pale outlines screaming for a hint of colour, a touch of depth.
Palette in hand, the wind as her brush,
a flick of the wrist and her beautiful land takes hold,
rich in colour, uncorrupted and vibrantly alive.

November 2021

Pasta shells

The advert read, re-location,
so brother, sister, cousins all joined together.
Firm in our mini shape like our beached cousins,
our bodies carry a lustre as we make ready to meet our new future.

First glances, as we traverse from dark to light,
I feel my own insignificance,
tiny in this vast tundra we know sit.
Lovingly you handle us, even offering us a hot bath.
I feel the subtle changes as my body grows,
relish the vibrant, pliable strength in every fibre of my body.

Strength in numbers they often say,
together we hold our ground, stuck together like glue.
Pristine white becomes our new home
but together we stand in simple defiance.

Hope is soon vanquished,
the first drops of molten oil and rocks fall,
shattering our resolve, displacing us from the horde.
Slowly we sink, our shells no longer strong,
escape a fast receding option.
Rising above the tide,
I cling to the pale yellow boats offering salvation.

Caught in the fury of the red lava, the boat disintegrates,
falling, I slither down into the waiting murk,
final thoughts echo in my mind,
MURDERER!!!!

They are my world
Promises, mere words,
never written in stone,
uttered casually and broken so often,
that they become meaningless and insignificance will surely follow.

As I skirted the borders of lies,
mired myself in gardens of untruths,
I sought a pivot, something to anchor to,
to build my hopes, dreams, and reasons for being upon.

My world,
now held in a distinct orbit by dual fulcrums.
Each emotion, decision, thought and all that I have become,
brought together by twin points of focus,
My world, my children, my all.

My mistake
Infatuated,
I placed you on a pedestal,
my goddess, my queen elect.

MISTAKE!

Yes dear, no dear, my stock these days,
dreams and confidence, gone, murdered.
Browbeaten, I fall at your feet, exhausted and broken.

The battle for the clty
Darkened waves criss-cross cobalt skies,
swooping down akin to the Kamikazes of old,
they alight upon remembered perches,
the battle for the city has begun.

The natives await their next advance,
feathers preened, they know the fight will be raucous and bloody,
the prime real estate of the city,
a fitting prize for the renegades of Spring.

Doppelganger
Why did you have to let her die?
That was where the end of my life began,
that singular moment when my faith died.
Did I speak out against you, mock everything you stood for?
Of course I did, what father wouldn’t.

The first massacre began after that night,
he stood there, staring into the camera,
mocking the authorities, the system, the world.
Speechless, I stare at the television,
I am there in full frontal,
there but here, no alibi, so the truth is pointless.

A game of cat and mouse begins,
the authorities chase their tails,
whilst twins of dark and light seek each other out.
Let the doppelganger trials begin,
the game of a petulant God to decide my fate.
Guess payback is going to be a bitch.

Broken crayons still colour
Shall they be discarded, thrown into a pile,
left to gather dust, forgotten,
isn't that what we do with things we no longer need.
Be it partners, friends, clothing,
all interchangeable on a whim.

Remember that pen, thrown in the drawer,
buy a refill, oh look at that, a new pen.
That partner we professed to love for eternity,
gone, not quite forgotten
but slowly receding into memory.

Shouldn't we remember,
did they not help mould us in some small way.
Things break,
in blind panic, we rush out seeking replacements.
A materialistic world, conditioning us,
telling us that we must replace,
Guess what folks,
broken crayons still colour.

<u>The wind calls your love to me</u>
My breath catches; I taste the scent of your beauty
riding upon the autumn squalls and dancing through my senses.
Seemingly alive, close to touch, yet,
remaining mere vapours coursing through my heart.
Each torrid draught carries a soft lament of your voice,
unspoken, your dulcet tones are whipped away amid the wild torrents.
Salient autumnal winds howl their laughter as my soul cries in anguish.
Upon swirling zephyrs each note is slipped beyond my grasp,
torn from reach, riding the silent breezes mocking my pain in whispers.
Calm returns, silence brings death.
My heart aches,
I long for the wind to call your name and
reveal your love to me in a forest lullaby

<u>The poet who cried</u>
stretching the void he sought colour
each flick of the pen
once rich in imagery
brought forth only darkness

Amid the tears, lamentable sighs escape his lips
a melancholy reward for the poet who cried

The art of the con
You want to believe,
it builds in your mind, suckling the greed,
filling your shallow void.

Misdirection on warbles of truth,
fortify the belief and obsessions of materialism seals it.
You never saw it coming,
never questioned the verity of their words,
revealing your weakness, feeding their strength.

As the facade falls, the truth is revealed,
Did you learn anything?

The Plastics
Every school has them, The Popular Kids
Warped humourless remarks
drip from poisonous lips,
bullying, their right of passage toward ignorance.

She knew they would find her,
they always did, daring to be herself,
mere catnip to the plastic hierarchy.

Tinpot gods,
allowed to rule through vicious popularity and fear.
Welcome to secondary school.

Destiny
Crushed under the unbreakable bonds of destiny,
the mind limps into death on the decaying wings of promise.

Loose Strands
Empire crumbling, secrets unearthed,
painted smile offering only stony silence.
Loose lips offered betrayal,
his dalliances revealed to unseen ears.

Loose strands erased in cobalt,
silence bought under a firing pin.
Regret was never part of his repertoire,
his shrivelled heart incapable,
smiling again as the bodies fall.

Brannigan

the first page turned
a young mind
captured, transported
thrown into the realms of a broken world
guns, lawlessness
littering the pages in blood
many books fell after that
each imprinting their will
capturing thought, feeding a thirsty mind
you never forget your first

rectangular boxes duly filled
hesitation, screen name blinking
hunting a creative spark
many names flittered
reborn, moths to a flame
seeking their place in my history
Brannigan
spilled from the blood of the past
rising to his place of honour
you never forget the first
not really

Daisy White

On a fragile stem,
pallid petals create a hem
around a sun of saffron hue
brothers and sisters joining too.

Swaying in a summer breeze,
family together across a floral sea.
Beauty twinned from ground to sky,
burning yellow in an artist's eye.

December 2021

Payback in fire
fear their weapon
across the popularity isle
rising from the ashes
memories feeding her smiles

tattoo's awaken
power unleashed
smoke drawing fire
to the breast of the beast

November (Acrostic)

november fell
overwhelming autumnal beauty in pallid colours
visual apathy arrived in shades of white
evicting autumn's terminal breath
man slips into waking hibernation
bombarding hope with perpetual night
enfolding the song of winter to their breasts
riveting hopelessness in nights of pitch

Winter in brevity
Silence.
Autumn squalls gather pace,
carrying screams of a season's birth.
Colour drained landscapes
await a virginal blanket of obscurity.

Temperatures slip,
frozen memories hibernate,
slumbering through a season.

Winter - A dark and lonely place
Icy blasts from the distant north,
herald the arrival of a brutal force.
Blizzards, gales, thunderous storm,
winter reveals its darkest form.
Robbed of leaf and early buds,
dying life, skeletal woods.
Battered hedgerows sit forlorn,
darkened smudges on a frosty morn
Pale, ravaged, a desolate land,
naked beneath winter's hand.

The night after yesterday
Cold, untouched, pristine sheets,
empty side, free of feet.
No tell tale shape like times before,
flattened sheets sweep the floor.
Pale grey light at windows peek,
relationship dead, no couple to seek.
Red rimmed eyes from a stormy night,
single in double a painful sight.
Tears dried since yesterday,
love in tatters, no more to say.

DREAMS
Forever in dreams the mind roams free,
emotions raw if the world could see.
Drifting blissfully we enter the sleeping realm,
our inner self takes the helm.
Steering us onto another plain,
life and dreams become the same.
Sub-conscious levels brought to light,
revealing hopes and wishes within a life.
Hidden messages lie upon the dream,
cherished hopes we seek to reveal.
My dreams, my hopes, I lay at your feet,
grant me now a peaceful sleep.
Be careful now, watch where you tread,
one step wrong my dreams are dead.

The Two Seasons of England
once as four they came and went
each different, alive then spent

in recent years they became new
leaving us with nothing but two
wet or cold is all we get,
it appears now summer has set

spring went first, simply disappeared
lost in winter, no longer revered

six months rain, now simply a bore
half a year left, with both at the door
wintry gloom rides across the land
no summer sun to lend a hand.

thickened cloud in shades of grey
embattled colours held in sway

Night at the pub (Barroom Acrostic)
beer glasses and tumblers rise
amber nectar, dark ales flow
roving barmaids drift till to pump
revolving doors, their coffin nails in the night
oligarch confetti greases palms
oppression offered in capitalist uniforms
mobile smiles painted till the clock chimes midnight

January 2022

The soul of Winter
silence falls in ivory hue
dusting footprints, hiding a few
winter's caress plays at the door
dancing shadows on a fire lit floor

arms entwined neath' feathery down
life asleep awaiting sound
muted silence across winter's sand
dawn awakens to a hidden land

whispered winds carried a jewelled repose
unique beauty upon a frosted rose
virginal white of a bride to be
loves embrace carved on winter's tree

Still thy tongue
Still thy tongue, you often preferred
childhood silence, seen not heard
in pen and paper I began to mend
embtacing my lady, my musing friend

I stilled my tongue as you decreed
an unnatural mute, a child not free
in her embracc life awoke
awash with words, we broke their yoke

my voice now loud ringing clear
unspoken words with nothing to fear
upon the page my lady rules
we have much to say but not to fools

Learning from childhood
throughout childhood I began to grow
laughter, friends and winter snow

rhetorical questions, the adult form
curbing language their chosen norm

elastic nerves born, tirades begin
silence offered, no will to win

impartial rays of unbiased love
offered to MY children, their hand in glove

Memories
Upon a page a petal resides,
red in hue, carefully dried.

A page per year we quickly set,
preserving love from first we met.

Many books have come and gone,
bookmarking memories of all we've done.

Snowfall
silence falls in ivory hue
dusting steps, hiding a few

winter's embrace plays at the door
dancing shadows on a fire lit floor

whispered winds carry a jewelled repose
unique beauty on a frosted rose

Casting a spell
magic
drawing earth,
sky, life, flight
tattoos awaken, power unleashed
tendrilled smoke wisps
skirting her
smile

Hey I'm walking here
hey, I'm walking here.

are you blind or just stupid
I'm six-four, broad-shouldered,
so I guess you're not blind.

oh wait, I forgot,
there are two sets of rules

one for you and your wannabe Nazis
and another for the rest of us

freedom
that bastard word
that still sticks in your throat
no longer hidden
beneath your boot heels

remember
try pointing the gun at the enemy for a change

Februaray 2022

For my love
snowdrops offer winters end
spring awakening daffs do pretend
then arose loves rainbow heads
swiftly filling tender beds

sensual bells begin to chime
warming breezes calling time
small bouquet from our garden true
tulip reminders of my love for you

The birth of spring
winters inpenetrable barriers
torn, ripped in her awakening
watercolour drips from her sword
igniting the rebirth of the world

thoughts flowing across her canvas
flowers emblazon her journey
carrying forth her message
hope

passionate in her endeavours
she sculpts art in exquisite masterpieces
lighting the way to spring for a world in rehab

working tirelessly from sunrise till sunset,
she reveals her beauty
the accompaniment of the dawn chorus
rousing life from slumbering hibernation

Muted

across brooding skies, the sun shies from view
lost behind battleship clouds ready for war

revelling in the birth of January
muted sound fights through air thickened with menace
striving to be heard from inside pre-storm deafness
no bird calls or children at play
disturb the murky silence of night on day

dampness holds ground in boggy disposition
ugly blackened scars cut across a pained landscape
grey wraiths blanket a battered sky
under weary sighs, we look to tomorrow

Monday - past and present

hl
i'm here again
Monday

weekend but a memory
relived in idle coffee chatter
littered with angry snarls of despair

I know you hate me
loathe my existence
yet
I feel the change
growing like flowers
rich in shades of strength

is this to be our new partnership?
my power slipping, yours growing
beloved Monday your new mantra
awakening something magical

Interseasonal
winter
the long sleep
broken

snores echo across waking buds
rumbling hibernation awakening hunger
the soft drip of tears
meets
the sweet sound of birdsong
first rays awakening
Spring choral frivolity
offering soft laments to the fallen season

interseasonal February draws to a close
canvas wiped clean neath' a March sonata
snowdrops, daffodils
embraced in the lyrical hope of the dawn chorus

sun dipped landscapes
awash with floral dances
drift on sensual breezes
swaying to the song of Spring
smiles rise in the realm of man
hope whispered on new torrid draughts

Nature's harp
gone are the frigid winds
Spring breezes call her from slumber
awakening birthing rituals on nature's harp

geometic artistry connects the poles
fastidiously weaving splendour
strings rippling in dappled sunlight
prismed dewdrops speak of rainbows

gossamer echoes ride vibrations
dancing with the morning concerto of birdsong
sun-kissed daydreams of supper
hopefully but a wingbeat away

The Real ME

everyone loves you
you walk in, whiplash follows
little smiles offered here and there
just enough to quicken their hearts
catching them all in a web
Lady Double P
pretty and popular
the winner without even trying

however
did any of you ever really see me
the real me

riding sunsets I fake a smile
under the cover of night, no need to hide
sleight of hand controls what you see
illusions all, not really me
outward repose of untainted serenity
naïve and broken, leaking purity
losing love at every turn
fading passions no longer burn
micro fissures releasing hate
eroding a heart ready to break

Floccinaucinihilipilification

worthless
your word for me
echoes of hatred spilling in spittle

Floccinaucinihilipilification
drips beneath by breath
vague ugly stupidity
criss-crosses lack of understanding

I smile, battle won
at least I can spell

What lies ahead
do we need to know
is the destination
more important than the journey

what will we miss,
as we rush to and fro
overlooking
when unknown becomes known

The day a poet and love died together
364 weeks I had survived
my eyes open, my voice clear
till you

pencil met paper with fury
odes of love, torrents of feeling
pouring forth in a legible scrawl

seven lines
one for each year I had seen you
confessions orated in HB lead
offering my heart with a shaking hand

disbelief freezes the moment
vision blackened, heart stuttering
each smoldering piece, torn
offered to the summer winds
blown away by an icy smile

the pencil lies idle, heart fallow
love ripped from thought
a poet disected
before I reached double figures

Repeating the day
another day closes
first lamps lit

lengthening shadows
places sleep on the menu
sameness colours windows
disinterest closes the curtains

The Insomniac
Senses dulled, anger rising,
same shit today, hardly surprising.
Pen to paper to flickering screens,
monotony waits amid forgotten dreams.

I ponder my part in this insufferable night,
eyes locked open, losing the fight.
A creeping dawn opens night's darkened shroud,
sleep a lost friend, now laughing out loud.

Awake or asleep, all appears the same,
overlooked by the sandman that never came.
No slumberland hopes, nor dreams of the past,
just the red rimmed eyes of the insomniac.

The failed serial killer
flickering sarcasm
cramps the the friendliness
your _oily_ facade
can _never_ quite capture

a _hamster_ in his wheel
forever spinning
wildless and tamed
by the society you abhor

anger rising, _burning_
belly squirming with hatred
yet powerless
as the day you were _born_

will you raise a footnote
the serial killer annals
lost in your hopelessness

My only possession
possessions
folders, meaningless digital imprints
a lifetime of ideas
adding to the grey in my hair
filled with furrowed brows, pain, love and me

a gift or curse
my daughter will decide
when she reads of my poetic life
traversing my journies beginning to end

worlds, characters, each rich in imagery
stories, campaigns to hold even stalwart players
will he see my efforts
incorporate them into his own
can he embrace my work
only my son will know

I have little
but my written life
is for them
my most prized possession

Displaced
winter
incarcerated in a horizon prison
spring awakening takes to the land

beloved snowdrops kissed the earth
when snow still hid the paths
heads beginning to droop
shadows closing in
their route to life blinded

brigades of trumpeting daffodils rise
displacing their cousins
eating specks of renewed earth
brought from hibernation
in dappled sunkissed shades of saffron

<u>**Happy Birthday Mam**</u>
Your love for us is an island
In life's ocean, vast and wide
A peaceful, quiet shelter
From the wind, the rain, the tide.
Bound to the North, by hope,
By patience, to the West,
Your tender counsel, lies to the Southq
And to the East, by rest.
Above it like a beacon light
Shine faith, truth and prayer;
And through the changing scenes of life
I have found my haven there.
One last thing is left to do
For this poem to have its end
A joyful chorus of I love you Mam
Happy birthday to my longest serving friend

March 2022

Night of the crazies

night reaches its zenith
they appear
lurking in shadows
faces, pale blurs under darkened hoods
watching me watching them
a flicker of movement
they lope toward my castle
battle lines drawn
a classic pincer movement emerges
separating under muted streetlights
frozen in motion I wait

a handle descends, a gentle rattle
eyes glued
a disjointed smile awaits my windowed return
face hidden in shadow
a broken landline offers no reprise
mobile coughs a death knell
lights flicker, die
my death warrant, maybe

shivers walk my spine
icicles of unease pierce my soul
and the game continues
rattle, smile, rattle, smile
under bruised nerves pre-dawn arrives
fifty yards
from work to shop
a venture I must undertake
headphone meds offer solace in favourite tunes

igniting a cigarette, I inhale deeply
first step completed
the door slams shut behind me
emptiness
simple night time shadows greet my venture
I feel no relief
still know you're there, hidden from me
lurking in the shadows
watching and waiting, hiding in the false dawn

Searching for Spring
Winter's putrid scent washes over the weary.
Hope rises on lilac winds.
battling with aromatic apple,
the fragrance wars begin for Spring's crown.

Storm clouds howl, creaking fingers lift,
funnelling life into baby buds.
Leaves erupt, soft murmurs betray their presence,
swirling life under a beating sun.

Season Change
Barometers slip, leaving ghosts of memories
imprinted in mercury film on a downward spiral.

Blue once azure, hides in a darkened hue
beneath ink stained clouds sullied with change.

Autumn fall arrives in a red spectrum
leaking the blood of a dying season.

Scattered entrails pirouette on frigid breaths
the new season bared in naked limbs,
dusted skirts reflecting early sunsets.

Broken nights

November began
Quasimodo twinned stances
echo winter moods

drab days roll on broken shores
insomnia a new friend

<u>**_And the spark dies_**</u>

he could feel the spark slipping
stuttering, not quite connecting
it's light slowly dimming

ninety plus years he shadowed the earth
a meat sack
complete with a new modern operating system

life held meaning in them days
impulses burning through synapses
powering the massive processor in his head

even now he could feel it dying
synaptic thought trickling
base codes from childhood the first to fade

his light is waning
death will soon send the final email
off switch depressed
spark snuffed out,
an empty meat sack all that remains

Scents of yesteryear

sakura whispers
catching scents in dewdrops

filling my glass
discarded flutes awaken
memories of yesteryear

<u>*Hello darknes my old friend I've missed you*</u>

Summer people love summer,
longing to feel the nurturing sun
caressing their bodies in sensual heat.

Temperatures soaring,
I wear an upside-down smile,
lethargy seeping into my soul from behind mirrored vision.
Months flitter by held in eternal light,
summer seeks its zenith,
under a final flash of colour
death seeks an audience.

I miss the bleakness of your vista,
the long darkened nights of your season,
the crispness of the air just catching my throat
as I drink from the well of plummeting temperatures.

I hear your song of winter amid the mournful cries of solitude
carried on skeletal branches reaching for the heavens,
a chorus of melodies carrying me onwards into the shadowlands.

Hand in hand we travel the night,
I look upon your blackened tapestry
and I wear a smile at your return.

"Hello darkness my old friend, I've missed you."

The ticking clock

Who are you looking back at me?
Our eyes locked in the seamless image of the mirror.
Your eyes blackened and weary, hair joined in plight,
under a slowly engulfing cover of white.

Gone now the smoothness of youth,
forgotten in the eternal battle of the ancients.
An answer I seek for this abomination I see,
deniability lost, for all I see is me.

The ticking clock lies silent some days,
my youthful visage returning to carry a smile.
All too soon bad weather has docked,
sending arthritic pains from the ticking clock.

Each second a warning, each wrinkle a sign,
age crept forward leaving nothing to deny.
Creak and moans of a body broken,
the fight continues till the last chime has spoken.

Passing

leaves caught in white
embrace Winter silence
as you did once
mirrors still echo your passing
memory ghosts whisper

Melancholy

ink flies
obscuring art in pools
aberrations surface

melancholy tones whisper
forlorn tears to the poet

Tracks of her tears (Acrostic)

Treachery hid beneath painted smiles,
Respite floundered, murdered in sun-kissed laughter.
All their sickly sweet mockeries,
Covering their blackened souls.
Keepsakes of barbed comments fester in her darkened dreams,
Shuffling her sanity toward oblivion.

Onward life trudges,
Faith, once a beacon, lies beaten, lost in the hopelessness of hatred.

Happy smiles jaded, joy long forgotten,
Everything she dreamed, broken.
Revenge, a tiny glimmer begins its hypnotic dance.

Tiny battles begin behind her tears of anger,
Each step gained fuels her new found strength.
All-out war awaits, is she ready?
Recruits fall into her shadow,
Stocking the army they created.

Under Yeats' fire

From Yeats' fire I pen these lines,
under Irish smiles I hope for rhyme.

From past to present we shall wander on,
drawing inspiration from Yeats and Gonne.

A love for the ages, infatuation too,
an entire love in a poem or two.

Terms of endearment whispered in many words,
under a banner of war he remained unheard.

Beauty penned in his thoughts of love,
poetry for the ages, a hand in glove.

Romeo and Juliet a continuance

Romeo and Juliet.

A classic story one may suppose,
but a supernatural twist I will propose.

A ghost story opens on Romeo's demise,
sweet Juliet lived, his final surprise.
Perched on high he watched her rise,
sword in hand, muttered goodbyes.
A lady of the night in cloak and gown,
seeking revenge, tearing them down.

Entrapped in love, neither ready to let go,
two souls became one, a formidable foe.

A bloodbath ensued, each family met their fate,
neath' the lovers' sword, death in their wake.
These star-crossed lovers are now no more,
revenge was sweet, cutting the poisonous core.
Two families slain, the rivers ran red,
final dagger drawn, all are dead.

Together at last, their spirits roam free,
lovers entwined in eternity.

Melancholy write

Stretching the void he sought colour,
each flick of the pen;
once rich in imagery,
brought forth the darkness.

Amid the tears, lamentable sighs escape his lips,
a melancholy reward for the poet who cried.

I loved you first

looking into your eyes
I saw love
with you by my side
I became love

the fragility of youth
costly misdemeanours
haunting life
warping the present

soldiering on unaware
my jigsaw broken
a singular piece lost
unable to be replaced
alive but incomplete

then I remember
I loved you first

The enchantment of nature

rising on lilac winds
aromatic apple teases the senses
losing myself
simple artistry
awakens the realm of man

knitted leaves offer a canopy of privacy
enchantment rises in a forest of beauty
feeding the philocalist

Knocked out of bounds

cleansing cataracted sight
soot fell
exposing a new landscape
filled with modern transgressions

digging deep
art exploded
constructing intricate webs
embracing the aberrations
he was once taught to fear

past to present
lines blur
traditional
V
2021
fear lapping at the edges

Dare You
chuckles on the breeze
my future or yours?
I wonder
she smiles
a new poet rises

A muse's passion

She's there, clawing to the surface,
hunting control, forcing her will upon his.

Alive to her whims,
strings tweaked, pencil poised,
the next assault begins.

Enveloped in passion,
words tear through synapses,
she needs his audience but not permission.

The shattered rose

Toward the facts, we first must turn,
if the truth we are to learn.
How this rose with body torn,
lies discarded, lost, forlorn.

Petals beaten in colours dead,
death revealed in a final bed.
Cast aside upon a lie,
when tempers flared on love's goodbye.

Crawlspace

Why?
questions echo as she climbs
does he grace her with answers
no he bloody doesn't
but his eyes deceive him
the wife

Buttercup summer

buttercups hold the hue
summer haze, beauty true

top to bottom a field of gold,
emerald stems standing bold

dynamic colours neath' azure blue
summer uncloaked for me and you

Reunited in the wind

upon swirling zephyrs
each torrid draught
a soft lament of your voice
reuniting memory and senses together

I long for the wind to whisper your name
revealing your love to me in a forest lullaby
born again in Autumnal beauty

The thief of time

He had come for the final clock,
they knew it,
the key was in the numerals,
he knew it.

He stares at the hidden prophecy,
slowly unravelling,
revealing its secrets to him alone.

Quickly turning the hands,
each new combination falls,
till the final click.

He waits for the spirals to equalise,
the feeling of euphoria to engulf him,
dragging him forward into the time stream.

Closing his eyes he feels his body being torn,
each particle riding the quantum threshold
straddling time itself.

He prays this will be the last,
the jump that takes him home
to the arms of his beloved Sara.

<u>*One year on*</u>

lost in thought I often dwell
upon the past, before you fell

one year on, smiles still shattered
truths and platitudes as if they mattered

small talk dies on the midnight hour
cocktails forgotten turning sour

silence returns married in pain
emotional torrents of tear tipped rain

the earth still turned, moving on
unmoved, uncaring, you are gone

with serenity and grace, you left this world
the rarest orchid, petals unfurled

I've skirted life wearing my pain
empty now, till we meet again

I often feel you watching me,
in my thoughts where you'll always be.

in the dark where memory resides
happiness tinted by your smiles

melancholy, my old friend
welcome home, do they still pretend?

Halloween anger management

the day is here
pumpkins placed
the mummy arrived
unwinding with haste

fangs bared was Drac
anger flared
witchy mama cursed
because she dared

boney came last
so often the case
he has no body
flesh laid to waste

together they meet
October 31st
Halloween antics
for better or worse

Bridge of dreams

from down the vale, he'd heard her whispered song
a haunting lullaby riding the squalls

with plane and axe
he set about his chore
weeks slip by unnoticed
plank by plank he builds their bridge of dreams

her melodious voice his drive,
the vision of her, his desire
with aching body and muscles burning
he lays the final knot of wood

into his arms, she dances
the vision he had longed for

Spin

fork-tongued truths
the politician's spin
lies their life
truth's a sin.

Bills

bills, bills, yet another bill
the cost of life left in our will

all fall through the flap
tidy in envelopes full of crap

all for nothing is my call
keep the bills change the law

Depression (Acrostic)

dangling on a precipice
emotions drown in numbed thoughts
precursors to the darkness
revelling in disjointed hopelessness
evocative thought consigned to a shallow grave
sanguine negatives to pockmark the whole
spartan comfort in wars of the mind
inner demons snicker
overlords, mired, rooted
no longer slain by a smile

Chained Equality

is my sexuality so abhorrent
are you really that afraid for your patriacy

remember **cha**nge begins with **cha**ins

your shackles may anchor me

but my words
can't be muted

Evening in poetic song
shadows creep, your face dims
matching my heartbeats of creativity
thunderous ticks betray your presence

mind churning
ink flows through throbbing veins
catapulting thought into cohesion
crafting poetic stains on a virginal sheet

evening bells chime
insect melodies pick up the tempo
a cicada aria bridges evening
offering thier summer song
to whispering careless breezes

the onslaught of night
grasps at windows
sound tapers, sunset falters
the curtain falls

Dust
betrayed in pockets of sunlight
specks take wing
falling
layering his work

new ideas
dusted flecks of the past
close the book on his work

Riddle me this
I am the harp of the body
where music may play

I am antlers on a wall

when death came my way

often broken, I self repair
what am I, do you care?

Foggy morning
I awoke with a yawn
to a windowed view of not quite dawn
opaque banks did descend
trailing wisps without end

horizon lost beneath the mist
day or night double kissed
sensually dancing to and fro
engulfing sight, moving slow

a hint of light burns the scene
true morning awakes free and keen
the fog recoils with little grace
knowing death had laid in wait

Firecrackers work in the rain
her fingers work tirelessly
interweaving jasmine and crossandra
tying loops
building her garlands of ocherous and white

the first rains of the season
whisper their journey through the valley
bringing life to husks
laid bare for their transformation

firecracker explosions shatter the storm
pods flayed with surgical precision
raindrop scalpels offer life
to your next generation

Painting your lives
stalwart we stand
playing our hand
standing tall
controlling it all

wasted breaths we're happy to take
leeching poison for your sake

in oxygen shades with air anew
aspects of life we paint for you

I waited too long
beneath skeletal paws
I began to write
recalling stories of my life

in ancient scrawl
my words took shape
some of love, some of hate

time grows dim, shadows fall
life in ink, captured all
final pages did arrive
a life in words said goodbye

Sakura Memories
sakura whispers
catch scents in dewdrops
landscapes healing under blossomed touches

filling my glass
discarded flutes
awaken memories of yesteryear

brief echoes

ride Spring's coattails
lighting life in tastes of beauty
falling swiftly
mimicking the fragility of existence

The snowdrops have fallen
lonely stalks
remnants of your passing
slips of green swaying in a breeze
sinking from whence they came
hopeful flowers have long since fell
pallid husks whisked to pastures new

brief was your life
hard knocks of season change
endured for all

neath' cloud canopies
shaded sunlight
highlights your birthplace and headstone
patchwork quilts of paled earth
soon to be gobbled up by the new

daffodil cousins orchestrated your death
strangling areas in razor tipped wild topiary
ushering forward their own coronation
ready to ride the Spring floral train

The fall of syntax
rules of language once proposed
modern abborations have now deposed
on fertile minds the weeds crept in
overthrowing tradition on a whim

snetences, structure still hold a formal post
enriching academia one can suppose
the poets woke, began to write
deleting syntax without a fight

tradition or modern, let it fall where it may
writing is personal, no more to say

Candlelight
Shades of night beaten back,
candlelight, wick black.
Warming flame for lovers true,
waxen images, firelight blue.
Empty night within a breath,
darkness calls souls to rest.

The midnight hour
Listen closely, do you hear?
The midnight hour's drawing near.
12 chimes ringing, the hunt is on,
ghouls to vamps all are gone.
To the surface they slithered up,
seeking souls for a simple cut.

A house in a glade
a house in a glade
dreams did persuade
a life to hold
built for the boldl
fading from view
morning anew
reality closed the door

As she passes by
sunlight kissed in darkened tresses
ivory whispers
intoxicate bewitch
echoing memories of her orchard home

onward she wanders
her lands captivated in beauty
Arabian Jasmine springs into existence
awakening neath' her hand
washing her passing in life

Off the grid

rats in a race
caught in a maze
towing the company line

awakening was slow
nowhere to go
out the logical choice

resolve began
deep waters I swam
seeking an escape

reality called dreams
or so it did seem
a house in a village was mine

dappled in sun
new chapter begun
off the grid I will remain

calmed smiles returned
health not burned
life my new living pen

What if I had changed

new
that was us
love infused breaths
flowing through veins of intimacy
catapulting us on journeys
through hidden cracks of differences

secrets
murky waters of gambling
a squalid moat neath'
my towers of lies

I don't hide anymore
fully embracing my role
the catalyst to our destruction

decades have fallen
tumbleweeds litter my past
yet I wonder
what if I had changed?

April 2022

Works written for American NaPoMo April 2022

This selection of works are the poems that I wrote during an event on ALL POETRY where I post the majority of my works. The event in question was National Poetry Month in America for April 2022. This was an event that required a poem every day for the entire month.

With Spring beginning to flourish, there are a lot of nature poems that look at the beauty that this season brings.

For more poems go to:

WWW.allpoetry.com/Brannigan Wordslinger

Steve

April showers
evening calls lights to spark
paled skies darken under an artist's hand

a twilight chorus carries forth the night
appeasing lambing storms of day

hail kissed rain in dappled sunshine
freaky weather announcing April's beginning

Touches
lives intertwined
billions interconnected by covert strings
all thrumming to beats of fate

yearnings,
inexplicable longing
caught on the wind
necessary meanderings
if destiny is to meet it's quota

Library closures
digital death came for you
non-paper brigades
counted time on your life
goodbye old friend

The Abyss
the abyss waits
yawning, hungry, inviting
opening my spirit for life like a can
offering shards to the pregnant thuds
falling through an uncaring, oblivious letterbox

do you think of the damage
the pain inflicted without mercy

mortality reduced to a number on a letterhead
your final epitaph for me
perhaps

Years fly by
April has opened
three months have fallen
a quarter of a year
I blinked and missed it

wolves remain at the door
baying for their pound of flesh

If I blink again
can it be Christmas
when goodwill breathes again

Springing forward
wilting slowly
neath' April's tireless winds
daffs know time is short
creeping late Spring blooms
whisper thoughts of future rising

sun soaked skies
awaken under changing clocks
intermittent raging clouds
offer downpours of growth
twins feeding in a floral circle of life

Wanderings
worn soles, perpetual motion
restless feet drifting through life
enduring occasional stops on life's highway

the itch always rises, tearing away expectancy
ripping roots away before they entomb him
the feet of the wanderer released

gaze fastened on the gold of the dawn
his path snakes forever onward
yet, he thinks nothing of the future
simply accepts the inevitable
a mere pawn upon a moving map

Politics
desperation
canvassers arrive in April sunshine
ready to spin their rhetoric

gentle drumbeats play on wood
warring parties of government
circling like vultures
day 1 cons
day 2 labour
blue
red
their badges glittering cold in weak sunshine

spiel drips from smiling lips
broken stares speak of futility

my own reportoire polished
disbelief widens eyes
I speak of constant failures
strip mining the middle class
building havens for the rich and politically minded
orations end in tones of finality
they slink away dejectedly

door closing again
I wonder if releasing the dogs
would have the same effect

Crimson Tears

under tight knit petals
dewdrops sparkle red

the secateurs cut deep
a simple snip
death arrives

colours
once vibrantly alive
paling in murder

falling
gracefulness spins in each arc
flashes of past sunsets
flicker across the grounds of your home
a final pirouette stills life

barbs cut deep
crimson tears pool
revenge served

blasphemous words cut the morning
your eulogy roared in angered tones
his blood meets yours
bandaged digits lift your lifeless body
a violent twist of fate
barbs torn leaving you naked

memories of bud to flower flitter in my mind
never just a rose for a buttonhole

Assisted Euphoria
Blue Lotus tinges the air
intoxicating
trickling across taste buds
exploding in euphoric plays
carrying my thirst
to your willing lips

bewildered, befuddled
I taste tea on your breath
fuelling carnality further

ensnared in raptures
I whisper thoughts of forever

After the rains have gone
pools
mirrored blemishes
caught in man's failures
betraying final resting places of showered tears

slated skies
uniform expressions of April
belie the sunkissed laughter of weekends past

bedraggled daffodils
raise their heads skyward
limping water bruised petals
seek the sun's bandaids

Rebirth
climbing roses
barbed stems hooked upon a fence
await an April coronation
flowers sleeping
mere buds hunt the sun
rebirth their new timetable

life awakens
birds skim the wind
hunting materials
buiding homes for family

new green shoots rise
emerald carpets seek a first trim
cloying scents clutter the air
Spring awoken at last

Barricades
existence or life
fine lines blur in comfort and pain

through triple looking glasses
I watch flowers bloom
birds, beaks filled with home
skimming April squalls

aching legs help me rise
knuckles whiten in grip stemmed tidal pains
twenty minutes shuffling a broken body forward
sit, repeat, sit again
onward the cycle turns

sleep seems an eternity away
and the promise of silent thoughts

existence I possess
life waits in the shadows
each of us unaware of the other

Last thing - every night

darkness
a single street light
illuminates my existence
shadows creep
hugging corners
whispering

a spot lamp ignites
focusing my pencil
dispelling their words with my own
brief clarity in a room of shrouds

sleep tugs at me
stifled yawns reveal failing time
the midnight hour falls
pitch coats to the familiar

crushed neath' wearisome thoughts
strength flounders
eyes flicker
I offer my body in repose
waiting for the whispers again
ready to face the onslaught of my nightmares
alone

First thing - every morning
nightmares
finished with my mind
recoil into obscurity
seeking shaded avenues
to plan and prepare for nightfall

dawn peeks, seeking entrance
light kisses golden drapes
floral prints ignited
highlighted in emerging rays

stifled yawns seek an audience
trampling through fatigued thoughts
knowing this day will be long

weary eyes resist focus
treacled thoughts build the headaches
so often poisoned by the light

pain flows through a triple windowed prison
maybe the nighmares are preferrable
my head droops in agreement

Masks
morning rises
the first mask of the day
slips easily into place
frozen smiles, eyes of mirth
bewitching in laughter

work masks are many
confidence, fear, disinterest
leader, confidant, friend
situational postures fill the hours
images of home flitter by

carried through the day
till reality meets hope

neath' moonbeams
night drifts lazily at windows
masks fall
and my true face returns to the mirror

The awakening of the daisies
sleepy eyes survey my world
6ft by 3ft, a windowed view
keeping my sanity alive

I still wonder at the beauty
swaying sleepily in warming winds
juice in hand I pause
spotting Spring dandruff
pock marking succulent verges
with white hemmed saffron buttons
littering as far as my eyes can see

memories of daisy chains and garlands
bring forth a rare smile
Spring to Summer
appears mere fleeting weeks away
a floral future for those ready to see

Sun-worshippers
mid-April
temperatures settle into mid-teens
the flood soon follows

shorts and long-sleeved cotton
orders for the day
14 degrees peak the mercury
sanity is burned in the first rays

I smile at your huddled passing
arms hugging bodies
leeching what little warmth remains
Spring fashion is of little use

to home you head
goose flesh raising hairs

as the cold seeps bone-deep
heating cranked to equal a Winter day

sun-worshippers
awoken from hibernation
meet the changeable sun of April
revelling in the cold

Painting words in starlight
stars rise, I watch
waiting for the change
picturing times and dates
you will see them through my eyes

my heart halved, rides the clouds
hoping to be carried across the heavans
seeking you in your new home
a world apart from mine

change fell in white A4
jobs, we had seen a few
wished for many
occasionally, a wish upon a star
bears the fruit we hope for

our old season rises, mercury falls
skies lit in pinpricks of the past
huddled in Winter finery
we drew our finger wands from warm pockets
using the stars, building poetic beauty
only for our eyes to see

clouded skies offer visual silence
my tears lost in staccato drumbeats
words washed away in failing moonlight

the heavans awaken
painting notes in skylit dot-to-dot
I offer my words
hoping you still remember
and maybe catch a glimpse through my eyes

time slips into apathy
a single wand paints the heavens

lonely, forgotten
writing ink in starlight
I miss you catches on repeat
only seen through my eyes

The tulips have returned
white on white held the line
winter enchanted by snowdrop time
brief it was before they fell
daffodils tolled Spring's liberty bell

standing proud like saffron markers
traversing March just for starters
twinned in sun, flowers tall
April may offer their final call

Summer peeks, temperatures rise
awakening rainbows in tulip bright
reds, yellows, lavender true
together in pre-summer with bluebells few

Daffodils are falling
creeping, crawling
strangulation cradles your final moments
headstones of lemon and green
hold your drooping bodies
death hiding behind rich life

withering husks fight against time
soon your burial will be complete
burned saffron awaits a breeze
offering browned petals
to a final ride on nature's airways
your place swiftly lost on a dandelion tide
till your next Spring awakening

Revenge
our past
tumbleweeds on many dusty streets

for me the hunt was life
a reason to still exist

straining at my lips
our story longs to be told

shadows danced in sunlight
swooping in decreasing arcs
circling our home
cutting through the smoke
to the remnants of my heart

one more dusty street
in a nameless town
your bolt hole

stepping to your door
a gentle click betrays my gun

narrative changed
our ending will be revenge

Blossom
explosions of colour
clothe bare limbs
non-ground based flora
offer their brief existence
as carpets for branches unready for summer

tiny flowers scream life

pre-cursors
show the start of a journey

before leaves offer clothes of seasonal green
from pith or pip
fruit begins in an array of floral majesty
apple, pear and cherry
creep toward harvest time

Changing the weather
darkened cloud of mischief
scud into the valley
whipped forward in tormenting winds

deep grey tinges the heavens
adding a twisted half-light to end of day
hiding sunset majesty from view

twilight awaits first spots
feeding floral bounties of Spring
offering a respite from winter stained sun

It only took two days
Friday fell as Fridays do
smiles rebirthed
lawnmowers, strimmers
add their whine to the cacophony of spring

verges gleam
haircuts close
spring weeds trimmed

Monday crawled into view
weekend antics slipping into memory
yellow flowers rise in abundance
lawns crippled
dandelions offering afternoon tea

Spring starbursts
vine tied stars explode
lilac bursts joining green leaves
welcoming Spring tides

Seasonal condiments
seasonal condiments
make their long-awaited return
benches, loungers
chairs no longer tied to boats
or the privileged crowds of the past

I smile at their hopes
sun with a hint of warmth
picnic blankets
removed from pallid goosed flesh
finally returned to the top of baskets for May
when the heated breath of Summer breathes again

Freshly laid Spring lawns
a spring soiree on virgin blades
upon a lawn freshly laid
no flower tombs, nor birthing beds
crack the surface or lay their heads
unbroken jade, carpeted clean
flower devoid, weeds unseen
till summer falls in disarray
Autumn rises, seeds away
infecting lawns with little sense
marring Spring one year hence

Dawn of the dandelions
jagged leaves of deepened roots
spray forth in abundance
rabbit meat flows from memory
drawing a rare smile on my countenance
nature's cheap answer for an Easter Bunny

verges riddled with dandelions
lemon yellow weeds
add their rich textures to a growing landscape
highlighting Spring/Summer floral splendor

for a world beginning to hope

April warnings lie in the winds
rising wicked April winds
tinged in echoes of the North
ruffle new found beauty
with caresses of ice

flowers dance on broken strings
praying for Summer breaths
single digits hold sway
April warnings betrayed in sunshine

flowers scream in whiplash
beaten, bruised,
heads forced to earth
bowed but unbroken
rigidly pliable
strength in survival

Trees are stirring
soft rustlings
new clothes of jade adorn
vibrant branches lift to the sun
undeep canopies
offer dappled life in shaded sunlight

brothers sisters sleep
unable to shake hibernation
buds unbroken by rising temperatures
unruffled in drenched winds
naked spined fingers still lift
awaiting a late Spring coronation

I remember

smoke drifted lazily in the empty bar
my heart stopped
I knew that feeling
had felt your smile before

the jukebox hissed its anger
our song reverberating in vapours
images of forgotten dances
bring forth memories
the sensual lines of your body
provocative moves highlighted in firelight

Nature's concert had brought us from slumber
wrapped in each others arms
beautiful tones explore reminders of a better time

softly I cried
born of your pain
feeding fears of life without you
and the beauty I tasted

our song ends
one more chance with you
I laugh
drinking till I see the bottom of the glass

stained and rotten from your touch
mere shadows of song still haunt my dreams,
constant reminders, when the sky isn't blue
it was you who brought the darkness.

Come with me
come with me
face your wish
take a walk
up the stairs of my mind

step by step
I shall reveal
beauty
darkness
me
tear deep
suckle on my hidden depths
embrace if you can

surprise, fear
shall take your breath
stop your heart
yet you hesitate
first step
or, is it the last?
welcome
to all that I am

My Final work for NaPoMo
pencil touches paper
thoughts ignite
carrying unanchored words into thought
floral tapestries fluttered, kindling scents
lexemes caught in brevity snares
drifting through Spring

April gives way to thoughts of May
the year's rebirth sung
I sigh, contentment awoken in rainbow shades

final strokes of lead

shake off the dust of a forgotten art
almost twenty poems carried nature's tune
one a day driving forward NaPoMo
seeking that fabled April 30
a score plus ten duly served
my pencil now idle
waiting the next wave

May 2022

Behind golden skies Summer fell
colour erupts
pastel shades of serenity
drift across the smiling throng of summer

easy laughter makes an early appearance
melodious tones carry hope
temperatures rise
the vitamin D clan spread their wings,
their seasonal misery
briefly tempered in Summer haze

beaten back under merciless sun-kissed days
cloud wraiths gather
planning their vengeance for season change.

east to west the sun carries time
ageing across the heavens
fiery sunsets remind the night of its brevity.

clouds swirl forward deepening their stranglehold
edges bright and briefly golden
grey visages lie heavy across the horizon
an unstoppable army waits

Tainted Sincerity
tainted words drip like poisoned honey,
mouth alive, lovely,
utterances of forgive me echo

disbelief catches my breath
voice sincere, you offer a smile
sincerity never reaching your eyes.

Does anyone really know me
kindly words from lips drip
catching in my throat
poison masked in perfumed scents

all-round nice guy
best friend, agony aunt when needed
all attributed to a wolf

if only you knew
I've never been all that

I never speak of my darkness
my personal hells
where I go to scream

friends I've forgotten
still faceless demons on media
trials I began and failed
still relishing that narcotic high

Twilight
weakened candles flicker to life
twilight snared in teardropped light
daylight stretched. clocks long chimed
eight now falls before darkness primes

hurrying home in Winter/Spring flare
hoodies and jackets still sensible wear
vests and tees still look to May
braving the cold of an April day

kids untired when darkness calls
begin their repotoire no longer small
silence waits for wakening lights
curtains to fall and whispered goodnights

Beneath Slated skies

nature lies silent
slated heavens mute life's growth
summer seeks the sun

Morning

dragged from sleep
tendrils of dreams, memories
replay in subconcious empathy

sight focuses on aging white
counting artex swirls
building geometric art
adding pastel shades on a smile

body screaming for movement
geometry still holds sway
slobbering kisses
swing my legs into escape
forcing a groaning body erect

through sleep drugged moments
I had forgotten
beauty is always there
be it a ceiling
or a four-legged morning pain
pouncing on the recently woken

Lost in twilight for a day

curtains pushed aside, dawn sighs
twilight begins neath' sleep tortured eyes

brooding skies hang heavy
awash in subtle hues
of smoke kissed life in fireless gloom

canopies of uniformed grey
close enough to touch but held at bay

onward the day travels
sun shards hidden from view
passage caught in digital tones

lost and away colours shy
May swung in on a departing tide

little change from dawn to dusk
insipid heavens to twilight took
ashen skies to darkness look

Sunbursts
sunbursts
braving Spring's personalities
I thrived in deluge and haze

my wishes caught in Autumn sun
wait to be blown
released into nature's airlines

Never truly on my own
caught in timeslips
friendships dwindled
alone the word I feared

eyes open
I look for my sillouette twin
a shadow Pinocchio, strings uncut
mimicking every movement
riding moonbeams with every step

empty seats surround me
I smile
knowing I'm never truly on my own

Tattooed Memories
faces tattoed on memories
mug shots of life and love
caught in smoke

one rises,
oil on water demanding attention
darkened lines speak of night
outlining curves of divinity
exquisite arcs roll from thigh to calf
baring provocative souvenirs
for life in singlehood

Dewdrop Memories
Daikan fell in throes
love dispels hibernation
dewdrops calm the sky
tears shed into memories
awaken hearts twinned in love

Groundhog Day
caught in a loop
groundhog day

kissing rogue sunbeams
eyes flicker open
body screaming
to flex, to stretch
wakening muscles from hibernation
pain ricochets
tearing tears from arid canals
tsunamis board the pain train

slow shuffles traverse rooms
incoherent steps seek a goal
juice found, snacks follow
doggy treats, a price for silence

to a well worn seat i arrive
computer fans whirr to life
building unseen links to the world

capsules, circles, land in my palm
liquid makes their journey palatable
painless promises mere hours away

click

my mind opens to tenuous tendrils
life linked in digital
screen named mannequins light the way
for a moment

Poppy
caught in tender hands
I pose for my close-up
never in fear of the reaper
your radiance highlights thought
gentleness allowing me to live
to offer beauty
lighting our path to Summer
together

Greensleeves
love grew without warning
a look, a smile, a lingering hand
entrapping my heart in infatuation
imprisoning coherent thought in captivity

dark whispers echoed
closing circles once open to you
usurping your place in my heart
How I miss you now
my lady, my love, my heart

One click of a button
the lines had fallen so quickly
words drifting on tsunamis
filling waking moments in sunlight
spilt ink, finger paintings of words
stencilled their place in this world

the whispers began
I had expected them
after all
this was my tortured journey

the assault was brutal
doubt cast upon every facet of my art
poisoned thoughts of the unworthy

the finger pauses
one press of a button
to end the doubts, quiet the whispers
delete?
click

Melodies
melodies,
memory reminders in silken whispers
caught on sultry tones

songs infected thoughts
2000 had barely traversed the fireworks
final bars of anthems droned into silence
two became one

tones darkened
pouring heartbreak into shots
with vodka chasers for the win
ballads filled the hours
questioning your role in a singular world
imprisonment without bars

Loose change
metal thuds spin heads to tails
echoing in a brass ashtray
discs glinting dully under a single bulb

scattered coins
change from many avenues
twisting across the fabric of life
each a memory built

a coffee, croissant
writing pads, pencils
usual Friday fayre

notes fell in silence
torn from a leather bound sleeping bag
music jamgles with each instep
caught on the journey of retail therapy

The start of British Summer
April closed on a breathing sun
lighting the way to Summer

ten days have fallen
blue skies masked
non-darkening cloudy of muddy grey cement
plastered across the horizons

small drops speak briefly
offering life till subtle winds tug
grimy dulled colours
belie the beauty that was Spring

Summer missed the valley when May fell
May began in paralyzed skies
soft drizzle opened umbrellas
hoods pushed upward
vanity kicked into overdrive

Summer looked lost before it had begun
shadows of Winter returned
pallid skin screams for the sun
awaiting the year's first free tan

Life often talks in riddles
talking in riddles
life speaks in many tongues
never offering completed jigsaws
the key to the lock imprisoning knowledge
answers entombed in coffins of choices

transparent logic
cornerstone of my beliefs
a pallid vanquished warrior
when emotion comes to play

At War
you're always there
speaking in tongues
clawing at the sides of my mind
flaying my poetry
crucifying words on a whim

whispers pierced armour
tearing at my chest, head
seeking the light
that gave form to my words

many battles have befallen us
wins and losses for both

years fell at every loss
a decade buried my pen
muting a muse longing to sing

wins
creativity burned
offering a lit match to kindling
words gorged on words
releasing my songbird
her lilting tones
finishing works one by one
before rubbish becomes the only word I hear

One Moment
skin feels loose, sickly
pallid hands, freckled
flexing fingers
athritic aches slow the process
nails trimmed, uniformed
small burn stretches
pain senors ignite
mind awakening, answers speak

I'm old

Dance of the wind
you fought for life when winter called
baby buds hibernating
wait for a warming sun

May winds breathe in bellows
battering fauna and flora alike
trees scream in torment
infant leaves wailing in unison
clinging to life in desperation
violent marionettes, strings taut
dance to the beat of the wind

twilight drifts quietening the howl
silence falling with the onset of night
gentle stirs flitter to nothing
awakening an evening chorus
ready to sing for their supper
no longer afraid of directionless flight

Bouquets
Bushels of flowers grow under your hand
Offering beauty in pastel shades
Unearthed stems meet the scalpel
Quietly crossing the veil into a satin tourniquet
Unloved under a capitalist tag
Everlasting blooms wait, seasonal orphans
Taken as an afterthought, re-homed
Sprays of floral confetti shall soon dust the windowsill

Where I live (Double Acrostic)
Evocative imagery shape a villagE
Saxon memoirs, history in circleS
Church centerpiece joins the idylliC
Open doors of friends, a momentO
Memories,laughter, smiles, caught on filM
Back when we hung out, before the weB

The heavens opened

warnings danced across two days
skies dripped blue pastel
pallid grey surfaced feeding pre-twilight
window patters broke sleep
briefly watering the wee hours

eleven bells broke the morning
the change was palatable
eyes drawn to triple panes
the downpour had begun

violent explosions raise puddles
swiftly pooling into micro lakes for a day
debris swims the channels
seeking escape in darkened drains

hours fall battering submission
flowers shredded waterlogged
Spring memories water-whipped
drowned in a Summer sky river

Floral Predators

predators
silently flexing leaves
creeping forward upward climbing
murderous tendrils seek purchase

daisies   buttercups   dandelions
all held the scythe
sunlight robbed and strangled
daffodils fall for a final time
mulch, decay, withering stems
a miniature graveyard
Spring's epitaph
food for thought

The poet
they looked into his soul
fear of the beauty therein
began the hunt
close calls etched ravines
still his eyes sparkle

wandering
neath' hills mountains streams rivers
hiding beneath masks of grey
his words still spill truth
works of eloquence no longer seek an audience
freedom born in passages ride a bookshelf
awakening the deaf - unzipping lips of the mute
liberty begun
all it took was a poet

Hiding in the light
peppered cerulean skies
embattled in white smoke
drift carefree
playing peek-a-boo with the sun

the man inside the glass prison
whitebeard sharp eyes
catching rogue rays of sun
watches May unfold its majesty

figures of the past present
travel well worn-paths
wonderment colours their thoughts
basking in the May light
heads averted
ensnared in their own lives
they look away from him disinterested

dawn to dusk

a figment from their past
hiding in the light
hidden from sight

Birth of a poet
they always loved to label him
obnoxious solitary often dim
they never tried to even see
nor to wonder what he could be

overlooked became his second life
precocious child to teenage blight
silence offered with every jibe
alone in corners he tried to hide

fake cruelty fell from his atrocious self
not hunting friends nor their help
rising up no longer lost
cementing his place paying a cost

thoughtful child to teenage outcast
he found himself writing fast
putting pen to paper he knows he's free
although ambiguous may his future be

Summer called
vests, crop tops, tees, carry the smile
clouds hypnotised with azure wiles
temperatures rise clawing high
Spring change a long goodbye

catching tans, green and blue speaks
following the sun day to week
forecasts, so often wrong
riding waves till the sun is gone

in darkened moods I simply watch
offering the rain they've forgot
shuffling away to a rear door
I feed on Summer

a minute
no-more

The Church
caught in sunbeams
a millenary plus change
stoic serenity in circles
a central figurine in a bracelet of trees

canopies offer glimpses
cold beauty of Saxon stone
ripped from a Vinovium fort
caught in windowed reflections
offering a prayer
to a door still shut

Sweet Pea
pink spectrums slide across feather stems
tri-petals of beauty tripled hems
meandering snaking seeking height
wearing sun-kisses before the night
dewdrop bruises spittle specked
caught in war colours flecked

seductive scents pale Chanel
addictive beauty casts a spell
enmeshed entwined summer's pet
walking cross canes through a net
fragile strength in vibrant hues
flowers of summer bright and new

Is it raining?
tarmac divots
on an urban golf course
add a water feature
from skies of dark

shadow rain
wispy forms fall in silence
blind to the naked eye

caught on the breath of summer

imperceptable shallows slowly rise
mirrors grow
emptied clouds frozen in motion
leave no sun to shine

Pollination
opening wide to taste the summer
glistening rubies awaken in dewdrops
seeking the warmth of a summer ray

unfurling beneath wing beats
thrums of excitement
send shivers through every petal

nectar waits a gentle peck
pollination princes dance to and fro
slaking aches on a sunlit morn

Selective butchery
three weeks fall, council returns
mowers, strimmers, money to burn
awakening tones of summer green
a floral barber shop makes the scene

my front garden awash with life
a wildflower paradise riding a knife
bluebells, daisies, buttercups too
torn apart under blades of blue

yet across the way old life stands
a wall above daffodil bands
remains of Spring join the crowds
unkempt, untouched, a growing shroud

wildflowers guillotined, a surgical death
beauty forsaken on Summer's breath
old stems lean with blighted age
allowed to survive in their gilded cage

preferrential treatment for the kings of Spring
life preserved upon a whim

Climbing roses
many suns awaken
dawn's still light dwarfed
in pocket yellows

shadowed greens
drenched in dewdop tones
weave vines intent on domination
intricately twirling mythical batons
inward-outward creeping
sinews crawling through the madness of growth

inward laid thorns
seek the unwary
a final stand against a wooden prison

Home ?
home fell behind your stare
back broken under none that care
step by step hunting the moon
cradling highways through tarmac dunes

free to live, not to hide
living life control deprived
decisions mine, a single thought
away from screams, anger bought

seeking new, a place to dwell
one of hope, not of hell
path lit in celestial light
heading for dawn to say goodnight

The wild poets' soul (Acrostic)
The wild soul of the poet,
hides under strained abstract,
evocative in meaning, simplistic in truth.

Whispers of identity travel in words, building
inner clauses to drift seamlessly across pages.
Literary vampirism, the aberration of language,
draws the final breath of the poet.

Pen to paper to bin,
ordinary dies in crumpled servitude,
enticing the wildness of the poet's soul,
to escape the strangulation of society, or remain
shackled to the mire of expectant thought.

Strands of inspiration twist into a garland of hope,
offering society's whims a chance to bloom.
Under the faint guise of normality,
laments of the past imprint on the future in silent screams.

Colour drained
shadows lengthen counting time
minutes talk in abacus tongues
twilight seeks a total

seconds stretch seeking another moment
colours dim fighting their mask
vibrancy frozen in muted shades

red seeps on blue
offering purple to the night
dragon wings crowd a western horizon

unlit by kisses of summer
life turned pastel after sunset fell.

The beautiful tantrum of the rain
ripping apart the Summer play book
warnings lit the sky
night fell on day
ten minutes of chaotic beauty
seeks to define a moment

a deluge seeks purchase
hammering ground once parched
trillions of geysers erupt
slaves to the wind

waves of sprey rise
catapulted forward
riding unshackled winds
to a final resting place

clouds scurry seeking escape
their deed completed
sun smiles
offer a tumble dryer to the recently washed.

Ice-cream
summer
jingles fill the air
a time for ice-cream
pretty dresses that smile
OH
did I mention ice-cream

Caught in the stillness of summer
no leaf or branch stirs
blue and white tartan
plays games of peek-a-boo
shattering the day

awash in colour
a sun-kissed afternoon slowly drifts
blaring life in silence
flowers stand sleepily
drowsing in summer warmth

stillness feeds the silence
emptying streets when BBQ's ignite

Missed a bit
strimmers belched
wakening whirring blades
cutting serenity in two

shoots pirouette
caught in brief winds
not realising they are already dead

rushing by in their haste
headphones drowning his concentration
daffodils embrace their long awaited culling

bald patches show soiled innards
slips and lapses
betrayed in apathetic meanderings

stunted green lies in uniform
perhaps not this time
toward the center a single patch stands

white confetti and saffron buttons
live to tell their tale
called missed a bit

Salsa or love
battle lines drawn
the first taste the catalyst
salsa, blood red
drips from her lips
vampiric smudges of ecstasy
cavort with lettuce, spices
tastebuds enraptured in perfection

in his arms she felt safe
wanted, loved, held in reverence

why did he have to force the choice?
was 50% of her no longer enough

decisions decisions
mind scrabbling for an answer
she knew goodbye would soon be uttered

Looking forward to the silence
light creeps over the horizon
the curtains of night open
dogs bark, cockerels crow
a village awakens to the dawn
a chorus of hungry mouths scream
flighted shadows begin the hunt

minutes fall to hours
baying hounds track each other
yapping, growling through windows
all and sundry in their sights
kids scream and laugh
lost in games of imaginbation
adding their innocence
to the cacophony burning into evening
feeding the headache begun at sunrise

twilight drifts like mist
shifting vibrancy to darkened hues
noise drones into silence
decibels dropping for another day
my dog sleeps for now
while I listen to the silence

June 2022

<u>Just another night</u>
another night falls
sleep forgotten
body halved at the middle
trapped, tied
an old friend on wheels
taking my midnight tour

pain pulses left
dripping fire into an old wound
drawing dewdrops
from eyes tired and drawn
unable to fight anymore

<u>My 50th year was nothing to celebrate</u>
sitting here aged 53
a friend's contest draws the past from me
to a distant time my mind returns
minus years of 3 I begin to burn

landing quickly in my 50th year
Covid whispers began to stir
a time of fear in my students dwelled
afraid were many of a trip to hell

soothsayers all ahead of their time
a new learning support walked the line
smiles of encouragementr logic too
I fought a bush fire with paraffin blue

the year fell, a world laid muted
death toll rising life looted
warning signs yet we waited till Spring

to build our battlements but death was within

no 50+ wisdom helped in that awful time
drowned in sorrow 3 birthdays of mine

Summer starlight
twisting tendrils of night
hang the moon on a string
I stare at silence
seeing a night without sleep

stars smile at the moon's waning light
realising their time is short
the long sleep of Summer days
is theirs for a while

Knowledge
the road to knowledge
begins with a single step

too little
the world flows in endless rivers
slipping effortlessly through grasping fingers
thoughts carried just out of reach

too much
pictures , ideas, become lost
torn apart on the shores of questions
life evolving into an interrogation of the mind

Raining all the way too hell
clouds
a study in pictures
mind running free
I saw them all
endless galleries of masterpieces
caught in the light of the sun.

subtle shades paint a vivid summer skyline
memories of past ages rise
cloud wraiths once roamed the sky
sculpting each cloud
into picturesque beauty for all the world to see

grey visages seep onto the horizon
washing away colour
dappling a monochrome canvas in battleship stains
no sculptures nor beauty just a barren sky

water whipped
lost in mists of lace
sickly scents awaken
cloying aromas an epitaph
stencilled in the rot of a dying planet
vexing the tribe of man into cursed insomnia

Summer line
tumble dryers languish
final winter loads dispersed

cables restrung post to post
airers turn circles casting cloth shadows
hunting the kiss of the sun

bikinis, shorts and vests
pastel to vibrant sway in sighing winds

empty of bodies, imprisoned upright
rigidly held in plastic shackles
waiting to be loved again

Of freedom I speak
freedom
myths tangled in persecution
implanted by warmongers
rich in falsehoods
reared in dystopian visions
re-awoken in oppression
murdered when bullets fall

thoughts enveloped in forced silence
dare we speak the F word again
or is it at last enjoyed by all
many say freedom is but a myth
liberty embraced when it's too late

Summer
living canopies shade the land
crystal beaches, burning sand
heated shadows shimmer and fly
swimming holes, sunburnt hides

pristine flowers in pastel shades
vibrant blossoms surf seas of jade
nature's fireworks in wildflower hue
disrobing summer neath' the blue

fertile lands teem with life
summer suns burning bright
sleepy days, starry nights

dawn explodes in radiant light

A night out but not for me
sunset kisses twilight
temperatures surf the skies
seeking cooling breaths
to tame June's cauldron

traversing footsteps I often trekked
friends amble by journey unchanged
iced beverages a bandage
to soak up the heat of the night

life is quiet
doorstep unmarked
everything abandoned
when I fell off the world

good vibrations under a smouldering sun
elated smiles from the world as one

Meal for two
petrichor vapours caress midday dewdrops
feeding my gift for you
alabaster orchids stand passive
picturesque polaroids
captured in a garden gallery
shadows kiss twilight awaiting the scalpel

soft vinyl tones caress alcoves
provocative sounds of summer
whisper in dancing gossamer ripples
awakening moods of eventide

seabass sizzles in lemon
coffin ready for a salad bed
salivating scents taste the air
fermenting tastebuds in textured aromas

seaglass tumblers refract sunset
burnt orange and garnet pastels
highlight sleek walls in shades of russet
mood set with orchid serenity
I await my love

The night that Gallinule burned
communications arrived forthwith
angel's ready, battle swift

co-ordinates from a spy in camp
fallen angels snuff the lamp

initial attacks in the blink of an eye
dragons swooping out of a darkening sky

outposts fell under the flames of war
retaliation a thought, nothing more.

annihilation counted in confirmed kills
leadership routed with fiery pills

triple explosions followed by four
under blood-red skies of a dragon war

surgical strikes with serpentine skill
devastation drinking its fill

fire raged from end to end
battle reports no more to send

ashen skies to blue have turned,
those were the nights that Gallinule burned

She plays to the night
tormented melodies fall from strings tight
piercing the veil with notes of night
calling forth in raptured beats
ghosts, ghouls, demonic beasts

music swirls with hypnotis trance
midnight's children begin to dance

violin concertos with added bite
bloodied trails belie the fight

twelve bells hollow ringing death
sacrificial screams in lyrical breath
dawn croaks warnings of broken light
offering slumber to the player of night

Sunrise
streetlights, mankind's earthen stars
add a glimmer to the landscape
a matchstick holding back the night

liquid shadows writhe and merge
draping buildings in uncertainty
a sombre dark night plays
unaware of dawn's awakening

in the east
white-hot pokers perforate the sky
each glowing shaft bathing the land

wails bemoan the cycle
shadows torn to shreds
the chorus of the dead
sung in vibrant colours

steadily the world wakes
yawns stretch the morning
unaware of microcosm wars
fought in the small hours

The dead wood
darkened shells deprived of life
lifeless fingers dark as night
tightened branches obscure the sun
vibrant colours already run
fetid air, a rotted heath
feeding life to a baby leaf
a single chance to be reborn
a wood not dead nor forlorn

<u>Sunset</u>

crimson rays
bathe the land in bloody shades
deep reds and pinks
add a strange alien hue
mirroring the red planet.

billowing clouds clot perspective
nature's bandages
failing to quell the end of another day.

blistering in abject misery
rose-tinted shades discharged
sunset falls into the arms of the west

night strangles the horizon
darkened shadows erupt
extinguishing all in their path

<u>This will pass one day</u>

I watched you crumble
blood draining to a chalky white
fingers numb, phone pirouetting in sad circles
slumping, legs no longer bearing your weight
horror disfigurement stencilled by a wooden voice
'she's gone' the catalyst of agony

grief and I are old friends
my inner memory echoes, this will pass
you won't believe me
numbness will be your cocktail of choice

beneath fused lips
I wallow in my own useless thoughts
watching pain-filled waterfalls begin
their fury bereft in racking storms of breath

there will come a day
when you smile at the sun
finding your place in the fabric of the world
alone and untethered
then you will know
she is by your side again

Lost sun
the countryside weeps
pale and beaten neath' slate grey skies
memories of baking bodies, sunburn and tans
re-lived only on overseas holidays
British sunshine lost to the showered mist

restless winds whip
dust and debris rise in cyclones
sodden clouds hammer all into surrender
a squalid heath their offspring

denim blues huddle inside windbreakers
eyes searching damp skies
hunting a glimpse of the mythical July sun
bikinis, shorts, crop tops
buried in closets
hands reaching for winter jumpers again

paling memories of sun-kissed bodies
trips to the coast or a walk on the beach
forgotten the day we lost the sun

Tumbleweed
wandering aimlessly
room to room
passing shrouds at every turn
fighting through the deafening silence

happiness
clarity clouded
how many turns, how many rooms
a tumbleweed in a three up two down
does it matter, no-one really cares

Dragonfly
electric blue betrays you
sailing carefree in the arms of summer

transfixed, I watch
arrows zipping across tall grasses
to and fro, riding demented bungee cords

grace and artistry hold breath at bay
zipping in stifled draughts
thriving in a solstice kiln
the hummingbird of the insect world
living life on the wing

weeks flow into months, mercury slides a warning
a mighty scythe cuts the sun red
frost pockmarks your home
a tiny light extinguished in Autumn silence

I'm Sorry
head drooping toward mother earth
panic-stricken
I tie your body to the cross
yet still you droop
deep red fading while sunset burns

is this to be your funeral pyre?
a sun wild and afire, angry at my pitiful efforts.

this shall be your longest night.
dawn arrives in subdued silence
has your wake begun?

my failure
a sharp pain to cut the morning sun
final tears of beauty flow

dewdrops slide down your paling petals
unseen rainbows join the lifeforce pooling
hideous shades of death in merry shades
one by one your petals fall
till all is silent and you are gone

a darkened patch in a world of colour
the untilled earth a final resting place for my fallen rose

The riverbank
tranquil beauty bursts with life
embracing mirrored reflections
crystal waters placate every waterfront
welcoming sun-kissed plateaus

golden heads rising
arrow-straight reeds mingle
wildflowers threaten domination
both seized in relentless quests for the sun

sailing on heated currents
plumages vibrant on an azure backdrop
swooping birds skim the waters
every day a quest for food
feeding rapidly growing young
a calling

rock pools overflow
life first tasted
amid hundreds of natural aquariums

the fragile beauty of the riverbank
victims of seasonal genocide
nature's scythe unleashes the floods
condemning this bank of life to a watery grave

Fire and passion
champagne glasses side by side
empty flutes content deprived
fire jewels decorate the room
ambient shades in a shadow gloom

sweat sheened bodies writhe in motion
bodies entwined in gratification
craven murmurs override endearment

empty words now the passion is leaving

dying embers in a darkened hearth
fading reminders of a fiery start
strangers in the morning light
fading from memory their passionate night

All within a day
hints of colour slice a darkened night
dawn stirs morning light
a slow-moving arc seeks the eastern sky
coaxed to life with a sleepy sigh

splashes of sun bathe the land
bewitching hues of saffron sand
ebony wings take early flights
sunrise shadows eclipsing light

heat haze, blurred images of summer
sweltering skies of unbroken azure
life living in every scene
noble flowers, grasses green
sun-kissed petals slowly unfurl
courtships painted in seasonal swirl

darkness charges, thunder cracks
lightning rips across the black
a tropical deluge of silver dewdrops
cast a net over summer sun lost
pastels skies painted in rainbow smiles
sunshine promised once in a while
blazing heat draws to a close
fleeing to the west where shadows unfold

a race across the skies between night and day
battle colours lead the way
sun-burnt orange of a fiery sun

the day's work is almost done
a blazing corona forged in radiant light
submits to darkness and the onset of night

Seasons
shrouds of silence under drifting snow
nature lies in an ivory gown
beneath winter's sleep, she weeps
devastation masked in bleached camouflage

her hands work frantically
springtime coronation, no longer a far-off horizon
her gown melts under warming rays
intoxicated the world awakens out of hibernation

a festive extravaganza of time
marks the slip of spring to summer
licks of fiery breath shimmer
fashion soars to less is more
months full of hope ooze from pores
barbeques, siestas, heavy lazy days
good vibrations roll coast to coast

autumn appears in mercury shifts
her array of colours hit their peak
masterpieces litter every avenue of life
mother paints her last
leaves spill in russet rainbows
torn and tumbled, disjointed pirouettes
discarded bodies rotting at our feet
her work finished she finally rests

winter tightens its stranglehold
sun cold and bleak
pre-ordained ruin unleashed

Too late to apologise
apologies, you've whispered many
be they truth or two-a-penny
why now should my ears bleed?
deafened with lies you dare to breathe

is it me you yearn to caress?
wanting my breath from neck to breast
an empty bed on winter's tide
candour or deception, both supplied

goodbye glued to lips shut
not wanting to hear another but
half-smile neath' your falling guise
au revoir slips, words die

to the open door, I can only wave
offering the escape your actions craved

FOOTSTEPS
toward the future shall we look
past mistakes shadow stuck
names, places, symbols in a life
losses, love, maybe a wife
children, careers, all appear
in a single imprint walking near
indentations feeding thought
possible lives we have bought

steps fade cruising alongside
flashes of life before the eyes
without warning they overtake
life in footsteps, death in its wake

Nightshift
oh to sleep, to awaken
when the sun caresses the horizon
facing the day with a smile
knowing night can equal sleep
sitting atop my wishlist
becoming a day walker
ink fading to blank

under grainy eyes, light dispels shadow
toiling I toast the remnants of darkness
the morning chorus, a cross to bear, again
falling across the verge of night and day
the hustle and bustle of a new morn, purgatory
each step a struggle fighting the demented day walkers

into bed, I slide
rays of sun batter at the windows seeking entrance
ethereal light illuminating a shadowed room

each chink in my blind armour
wedging my eyes open
sleep an absent friend
stifling a yawn,
a rye smile counts fallen days

Life below the surface
reaching for the sky
stretching, seeking sun, rain
your search for life, constant

I reveal little
waxen leaves, shade from your precious gifts
thriving where your seeds fear to land

spiced with salt

a miniature Atlantis teems with life
secreted in rooted security
the mangrove, open for residence

One night
dusk settles
shimmering colours awaken
edges reach stark reality
holding for the briefest moment
rebirthing a shadowland

black velvet seeps into the horizon
silken gowns slip across the day
heralding the descent of night

light held at bay
seasonal time is fleeting
night seeks dawn
pursuing one more moment
battle lost, shadows concede

sunrise rides in triumphant
darkness dies in a bloody swathe
a light parched land awakens
starting a bright new day

Brief Encounter
bathed in rainbow shades
neon caresses the contours of your body
painting sensual arcs in vibrancy
licking your lips with a sensual tip
you offer a smile
desire rises in my chest
turbulent, savage
breath catching, dancing in hunger

dawn awakens
the maelstrom of wantonness replays
parasites of guilt plague conscience
heads bowed we slope off into the morning

our time a solitary echo
soon discarded
lost in that fleeting moment
when time stood still

Winter views from home
thirty-five years have passed I walk an unchanged vista
pale, beaten fields as far as the eye can travel
meadowlands, broken intermittently with gorse and trees
natural barriers in frozen splendorous beauty
stark greys of winter cannot diminish
the true beauty of my forgotten countryside

birds of winter pedigree flock
dark smudges upon a monochromic backdrop
the magpie waits, our own black and white native
eyes fixed intently upon the gold of the dawn
ducks glide over glass waters, unimpressed
paired until Spring swells their ranks
their life caught in seasons to be endured

soft shallow gurgles hide faint echo rings
jumping trout inexplicably drawn upstream
hunting traces of spring spawning grounds

visions of home caught in a masterpiece
pastels running in obscuring rivulets
perennial rains, battering, nurturing
carrying winter screams over hill and dale

FORGOTTEN BEACHES
pristine polaroids, postcard stamped
junk and trash, nature's tramp
her gift despoiled in the age of man
nature weeps, fighting all she can
deserted, abused, scrapped grains of sand
unkempt, forsaken, a forgotten land
footsteps lost in past mistakes
dying holidays begin their wakes

The year the rains came and stayed
November slipped into December,
winter began its reign.
The cobalt blue of summer cracked
revealing the cancerous innards of a season's death.

Erupting across the horizons
battleship greys join in unity,
warning of weather extremities
ready to befall man.

First spots soak into water starved ground,
greedily, hungry for life, shoots reach for the missing sun.
Sheets of rain hammer resistance,
under hooded brows man stares balefully at a liquid sky.

Noah stirs, his record broken, drowning in a water whipped world,
forty days long surpassed under thunderous skies.
Shrugging into coats man soldiers on,
summer a fading memory, briefly alive on postcards from the edge

Whispers

oh my smoky apparition
soft, alive, awoken under ghosted touches
a night in sleep
in dreams
in love

grey light creeps through a darkened night
I love you
a final whispering echo
thrown from the realms of memory
longing sated for a brief moment

your whispers caress the night
awakening the hairs upon my neck
again

Whispers in the night
mind rattled straining for cause
building sighs, diseased flaws
echoes from crossed radio waves
mind a flutter in coffins and graves
reasonable answers my mind suggests
ditched one by one, at its behest
creaks ring on silent stairs
strangled musings on frozen air

whispers caress the night
building fear causing fright
undiluted utterances molest my mind
psyche bruised, midnight chime

non-sensical trash no longer sought
understanding unlocked the door
revealing answers I was ready to grasp
not of science, paranormal perhaps

bathed in murmurs from a muffled room
dash of winter under a warming moon
white plumes of breath expose your essence
shrouds of shadow hide your presence
I feel you there, hanging near
just out of shot, muddy clear

frozen kisses walk my spine
riding shudders, is this my time?
gripped in arctic breaths of night
five hours must fall from midnight to life

Storm

raindrops cascade
tiny rivers of pearl seeking a destination
each reflection, luminous in crisp neon lights
false allure amid the deathly calm

angel wings beat to herald the storm
forest creatures' senses alert
seek refuge to quiver and hide, fear rife
thunderous echoes reverberate
distant drumbeats conducting the storm
white-hot thunderbolts singe broken skies
pungent odours catch in the throat
unshackled scents of putrefaction
quivering aromas of death

salient winds into a frenzy fly
speed, momentum
all hungry for the chaos promised
a pillaged land in its wake

indifferent to the plight of life
the storm moves on

A day in the life of my daughter
I wait
over stimulation, eyes flashing why?
hand-drawn air images on the fly
fighting your demons, trying to flee
words arcing into a stammering spree
twinned in knowledge we freely speak
hunting enlightenment I let you teach

I watch
masking soldered into place
hiding yourself for public grace
from foot to foot or in a seat
your happy dance an internal beat

I look to the past with shameful thought
missing all that you had fought
trying to grasp your personal hell
ashamed, I've no more to tell

(Written about my daughter's battles with ADHD and Dyspraxia.)

You are my one regret
my first mistake
you smiled
I noticed
easy prey
drawn in behind eyes that twinkled feline

mesmerised
predator and prey
swaying in practised sultry steps
laughter choked intimations drop my guard

there had been stories, whispers
your bitter corpse riddled past a highlight
conquests smirked just out of earshot
but your grip was tightening
escape a fleeting impression

things we did still hang my head
body soiled and wilted

yet you show no humanity
the easy chuckles of the victor
drip from lips still red

drunken nightmares hold reason at bay
fog-filled avenues of one-way streets
blacken the sunshine concealing the clarity I seek
to drag the truth to the surface
so I can recollect
you will always be my one regret

The music box
thrift shops and flea markets
your mantra
recycling junk treasures
your passion

a teak box
followed you home you said
a chuckling smile winning the day

lid popped open
Fugue echoes
mimicking your ballerina
you dance

I watch perfection.

First time I saw you was in a dream
sunset slips into the waiting arms of night
the sizzling heat of mid-summer stuttering

tired legs seek my own solitude

soft halos of light
frame the vision before me
rooted, I rub my eyes for clarity
soft eyelashes accentuating your beauty
twin pools of emerald seduction stare deep into mine

feather rays of moonlight
ruffle dark tresses of ebony
moonbeams wrap around her body
bathing shapely lines in liquid motion
offering the goddess elect to my sight

"hello" slips enticingly across the breeze
taunting, tantalizing, whispering
tangling your breath in my senses

gasping,
images of exquisite symmetry slip
lost in the realm of dreams

At home in the night

I'm alive in your realm
longing for moonlit caresses
intoxicated with darkness

the disfigurement of my rotten core
stirred
liberated
daily camouflage shed like a second skin
I rise from the shadowlands
becoming me
the dark wraith drifting on the breeze
indistinct among the shadowed views of night

dawn rises heralded in song
the painted mask of the daywalkers returned
hints of normality to quieten wagging tongues

Indulgence

backwards forwards folding

rising flowing escaping
a slow-moving waterfall ebbs forward
obscuring a firm globe of divine inspiration
gently steaming in adoration of perfection

glinting in candlelight
steam tinted, the kitchen guillotine falls
scooping away mere centimetres of magnificence
taste buds awash with desire
breathless sighs of contentment explode
firing degrees of repetition
offering the last grasp of toffee-tinged chocolate indulgence.

Moored

casting a glance
sunset kisses the horizon
my hand salutes

life on the water
broken with age
a land dweller anchored
heavy boots traipse to shore
moored in twilight

Hello Summer

sun-kissed cerulean skies
sixteen hours unbroken
the mythical June sun, no longer a fable
Summer has arrived
the searing heat of triple digits
wearisome thoughts on day one

gentle breezes caress napping leaves
mercury slips to balmy nineties
whispering lullabies for the drowsy mind

flowers bloom, colours explode
the buzz of industrious insects
the hungry squawks of new young
circle of life begun

with a smile, I whisper
"Hello summer" afraid to break the spell

To be children again
hours slipped by unnoticed
sunburnt bodies
lanky streaks of bacon on bone
unruffled in heat shimmered July

hayfever riddled scents
drifted from freshly mown grass to air
sniffles and sneezes tempered
dancing to the beats of restless thoughts

arcing across the azure
the sun, low-slung, hung just beyond reach
we stretched stubby fingers
perspective, a foreign word to us

memories
when the air was sweet
warmed with the breath of summer
our season

It matters not
that thou art blamed shall not be thy defect
education reveals the child imperfect
private handshakes and coded ties
versus public stigma with callous sighs

Shakespeare speaks from both gilt and tatters
the flow of words all that matters
ink on a page can unlock the door
students the key for classics to soar

a son of a glove-maker began these words
educational gifts he did observe
a love of language and beauty therein
weaving ideas upon a whim

it matters little what ignites the flame
public or private the subject's the same

Eventide

sun slipping, heat dwindling
night's dank bandages slither across its face
the battle lost
man lights his lamps
the funeral of sundown lit in electric tones

icy fingers of sunset caress my arms
seeking entrance
never quite grasping
the relief from the kiln of summer
offered in eventide

From the mind a poem is born
letter chains drift in smoke
seeking adhesion
snatching words from banks of life
lines flow into stanzas
emotional tinges crystalize
sinking roots in poetical symmetry
a muse's approval
frees the mind of the poet

Summer nights
pores drip inks of summer
midnight digits hold the day
cradling high teens before the rise

muggy nights seep into horror
air hands tighten and loosen
whispered coughs caress the wee hours
carried in degrees on passing breezes
eyes red, clothes tighten
sweat plastered cling film
bound in a stranglehold of insomnia

sunrise creeps in apology
first coffee in hand
a heavily caffeinated day begins

Abstract spider
raindrops nestle caught on strands
a snapped thread here, a gaping vacuum there
geometric oddities caught in a web
answers elude me
wind whispered storms
tugging at loose ribbons rises to the fore
lines of inquiry perk my interest
puberty's burden, the curse of the young
discarded as you idle in a corner
not quite an ancient
but no longer a feisty youth

blemishes catch my eye
arachnid quirks
the foibles of the true artiste exposed
the world of an abstract spider
revealed in offbeat symmetry

Me
closeted memories lit the way
drooping smiles every day
childhood introduced my motto
care for nought not even tomorrow

little boy lost a modern meme
survival a question until sixteen
branded thief, vandal and liar
knocked me around to douse my fire

my passion was strong from the start
no regrets, I readied to part
quill packed, I'm standing tall
despite your efforts to crush it all

friendship a gift, an inner peace
building a palace you couldn't reach
fear and pain in an isolated past
living each day, is it my last?

time's caught up, my poem is done
have I finally won?
closure I bought, shouldering a fee
that began in pain and ended in free

Views from my summer window
triple panes his line of sight
heat hazes dance beguiling life

people watching, through windowed sighs
reflections caught in peppered skies

seeing the past, seeing himself
walking idly among nature's wealth

threefold windows, a prisoned view
never to taste a summer's hue

flowery gardens shaded bright
medication for wearied sight

triple panes darken, lamps lit
birdsong echo their goodnight kiss

Old Man
whitened flecks replace the grey
wrinkles added every day
leathered skin, bruises fade
fighting the world, prices paid

belief and strength begin to wain
time fought, darkness slain
returning to life from the cold
smiling mirrors reveal the old

The Berry
orange swirls in a breeze
berries bob on seas of green
rich pickings in a summer kiln
times of plenty, a living film

birds land with elegant grace
designer fauna with a berry glace
feeding frenzy, hunger sated

food for life, berry tasted

starvation and scarcity soon appear
deep-set promises from winter I hear
fighting the elements every day
hunting food in every way
wishing the months would finally hurry
till rich new life heralds the berry

Life through a lens
photo-sensitivity, life in a sneeze,
caught in shades, from spring to freeze
cloudless skies, wearisome sights
sunlight endured till the falling of night
sunglasses returned from where they came
knowing tomorrow will be the same

beneath dark clouds or stormy gloom
unshackled eyes gleam flowers in bloom
rain starts to fall, offering a chance to see
natural beauty from blooms to tree
life through lenses in a darkened hue
or maybe behind mirrors for chances are few

Dream Lovers
dancing through memories
our minds flit across the membrane of sleep
unable to pause, onward we travelled

across oceans of time, we swam
bathing in passions from yesteryear
catching our breaths on the shores of hope

reality became a byword
quickly lost in each unified heartbeat
moonlight serenades drifted through our thoughts
entangling bodies in shades of the forgotten

Sleep - If only
hello old friend
is it time?
I await your embrace
to carry me onward
into the realm of sleep

a grin belies your true intent
a sharp turn of foot
flurries of coat tails
whisking yourself away in glitter rain

eyes drawn into silence
head sagging, views misted
a return to the usual beckons
insomnia

Butterfly brevity

wings unfurl
a brevity of life begins

gliding currents of summer,
beauty, stark, real
drifting in shimmering heat hazes.

Age of innocence
just a laugh
hints of make-up
lips pouted neath eyes that sparkle
commodities to feed their avarice

an age of purity
corrupted
society seeks perfection
age becomes irrelevant

Life - a study in monotony
I miss the sense of ambition
goals caught in singular thoughts
university, career, family
building a presence in this world

any purpose now is preferred
before I choke on tedium
become a leaf on the breeze
a mannequin on a bench
watching life stroll by in dying minutes

life eclipsed
shadow thoughts in a silhouette reality
monotony, a new best friend
dining on the periphery of life

July 2022

Seasons change in one day
a season's hopes travel June to July
fire and ice on the English isle
within a day both appear
diamante sparkles, Jacky Frost's near

muggy humidity a mosquito haven
blood suckers united seems almost craven
steadily in earnest gardening starts
under simmering heat weeds depart
replaced by flowers soaking up the sun
petals unfurling, a battle won

on the horizon, dark clouds amass

anger and fury rolling forth and back
unchaining the heavens the violence hits
lightning strikes, flowers in bits
torn asunder by a summer storm
shredded petals lie forlorn
light appears; the sun sneaks a peek
a river of death on a seared heath

The Fog
across each field
creeping nearer, edging forward
white plumes drifting in early sunrise

frozen shoots of winter grass left in its wake
a slow-moving opaque bank
climbing relentlessly over paths, walkways
seeping across dale and village
seeking entrance into the land of the living

a hole appears, another follows
you recoil
shifting from opaque to transparent
torn and shredded by the waking sun
each ray of October light quickens your retreat
sending you scuttling back to your home

the river flows into sight, unmasked
re-discovered under your dying wisps

akin to Dickens I watch
knowing tomorrow you may make it to my door
sucking the breath from my breast to join yours
sunrise failing as my saviour

Dare You
wandering through meadows of creativity
questions bark
should he stop
take the time
sharpen his quill
become more than they branded him
wordslinger

poetic vision rises from the dust
tired fingers reach for his quill

dare you?
his muse mocks him in question

Shadow Father
belligerent father, three steps ahead
shamelessly wishing to be anywhere else
but amid his partner and children

children underfoot, by their side
wearing smiles that lighten darkened days
blessings overlooked in spiked phonetics

polyphonic warnings echo in sunlight
hands fumble pockets
amid weasel glances and monologues

suspicion rides a Nokia
probing insinuations cut the day
mistrust overrides social etiquette
decibels rise quietening children

airing their dirty linen on life's washing line

pleading fake innocence
father and family wander on
lost in arguments, heading for home

Sharp learning curve
nest
pushed
plummeting
flight - well hopefully

ground rushing up
diving into technicolour clarity
this is going to be close, very close

wings unfurling, heart hammering
she catches the first eddy
leaves erupt in tiny hurricanes
gliding through her dust cloud, she rises
wings flapping to match each heartbeat
bellowing a raucous scream of victory
she soars to new heights

A dying world built on lies
insight
catnip to my logic

the world dances on a precipice
news cycles poisoned
turgid lies cavorting with pallid half-truths
mockeries distrust misinformation
scattered orations on the political landscape

Covid ravaged the country
Partygate and Beergate surfaced
seething contempt of the power-hungry
discarding rules, obligations
smiling as the world died

the world turns

broken, unbalanced, rocking on its axis
anger burns, masses restrained
politicians the new enemy

Cold snap
night collides in perpetual motion
engulfing the land in frigid breaths
temperatures slip
minuses hold court
diamante sparkles wash roads and hedges
ashen trails of the cold snap

I smile
people huddle, lost in deep down coats
senses numbed under billowing layers
icy shivers ejected in feathery gasps

faces blur
hiding under masking scarves
the true allure of winter
lost in tropical reveries

Memoirs of a serial killer

blood flow numbed, a knife embedded
my inner devil sniggers
waiting for that extra gram of pressure
then the gush

sharpened edges slip free
and euphoria is upon me
each scalding drop an instant high
narcotic hits of exalted proportions

sadness surfaces
she's not the one

patiently I perfect my art
many days have come and gone

waiting for the sun to sink
many nights followed
watching them all from the shadows
the wraith in the night
bathing in the blood of doppelgangers
living in still moments
till the time is right

watching your pale silhouette transform
each layer falls until you bask in naked divinity
flowing through the shadows I begin the hunt

silence lies upon me
countless dreams have courted me
their raw scents of fear my elixir
salted tears my ambrosia

from the night, I arrive
turning the handle
my smile broadens
feverish eyes lighting in mirth
silly - silly - girl
I must remember to thank you for the open invitation
the door snicks closed behind me

Dark Storm

1010 a.m.
storm clouds easily obscure
a summer sky briefly azure
darkness seeps with a heavy sigh
salient winds into a frenzy fly

feuding clouds hold the line
waiting storm calling time
children's faces, ashen white
pale and worried in a day dark night

words of comfort quickly gone
lost in echoes from beyond
peal after peal beats the lonely drum
explosive lightning adds to the hum

bundling my kids into my waiting arms
onrushing torrents break the calm
legs pumping hard, I head for home
lashes of rain mask the sun
running swift to stay ahead
through the door with slackening dread
rain smacked windows tell the tale
heavens opened over hill and dale

The song of winter
haunting tunes play upon stark white tapestries
sheet winds sing icicle melodies
screaming branches resonate in skeletal tones
musical interludes on blackened street mirrors

arced sunlight barely rises
diffused off-handly under a leaden sky
shivers ripple across the land
people snug in many layers
balefully mutter to the skies

I feel no cold
losing my thoughts in the sounds of winter
set adrift in dreams yet born

Darkness falls
darkness descends
dark brooding shells of buildings
stand darkly tall in menace
murky shadows alive and waiting
behind windows silently opaque

street light ambience pales into insignificance
shrouds of darkness seeking to engulf all
allowing the night to reign supreme

cracks in pavements yawn grotesquely
vain attempts to entice me
yawnings widening to their shadow realm

hunting always hunting
the darkness feeds upon my fear

sleep dwellers unaware of my dread
walk the same streets in nightmares
this darkest of walks home
bruising every nerve
sending icy tendrils snaking up my spine

flooding rooms with homely light
leaving the night clawing at windows
I desperately hold back my terror
petrified in this darkest night

Pathways
restless winds through branches whistle
stirring leaves in persistent motion

trees murmur a requiem
at the wind's relentless torment
pretty flowers adorn every path
silver streams sparkle in the distance

pathways crisscross
fields of deepest green
whispers of summer
capture the music of the walk
I give you my England

The last flower
alone, swaying in a breeze
forgotten, lost, no longer seen
summer to autumn seasons slide
colours lost in mists of time

no petals, nor leaves, a stalk sways
clinging to existence in darkening days
neighbours gone returned to the ground
children whisked away without a sound
riding the breezes as you did once
to pastures new, for a springtime dance

battered and bruised by winter squalls
slowly you droop, heeding nature's call
mother earth rides in before winter's tide
final lights ebb and die

preserving nature's machinations
returning you home to hibernation

New life
climbing roses, barbed stems hooked on a fence
flowers snug in protective buds await early April
spring's nurturing sun their key to freedom

birds returning to these shores
work feverishly constructing new nests
ready to greet the arrival of their offspring
newborn young are soon ready
to take their place in the circle of life

young green shoots rise
carpeting barren lands in new life
the scent of freshly mown grass
sickly sweet and cloying permeates the air
rich scents released in rainbow pastels
bees and butterflies arrive for an early pollen test
heralding the true arrival of spring

Summer Love
twilight adds a luminous cast to her hair
darkened tresses alive in sighing winds
hiding the tears she weeps

haunting lullabies caress sea breezes
creating lyrical whispers to their summer of love

a final walk
brought swiftly to a close
by the hands of distance and time
memories eased out of existence
by the rebellious breakers on the shore

Tramp

rheumy eyes look belligerently upon his world

worn fatigues hang loosely on his frame
abnormally thin, twisted and lame
dirty nametag lies faded and worn
a reminder of a proud life, tattered and torn

holding out his grimy paw
shadows falling on his dirty floor
a scowl cracks his dirty beard
sunken eyes betray his fears

unruly hair wild and mad
hides the sadness of what he had
a bewhiskered face walks the past
haunted memories moving fast
ghosts parade this better life
riding the edges of a mental knife

One last look
through rays of sunlight dust motes dance
vibrant and clear upon a glance
each speck a memory, again alive
shadows past cloud his mind
upon a touch, all returns
kids raising murder at every turn
a smile from his wife that could light a day
blinding memories of what happened that day

pain rising aching to be free
everything gone, all he can see
the present returns to a derelict waste
nothing left, sadness laid in wait
one last look was all he sought
drifting away, his final thought

True love
passionate murmurs whisper sweet
soft lips brush her cheek
opening eyes to ecstasy's embrace
awakening desire in sapphire shades

feelings, desires, burn inside
seeking togetherness, riding the tide
merging, entwining, two souls become one
coiled in unity their eternal song

love a paradox some never find
many are blessed to find it first time
love's a hard taskmaster if you build it to last
remember mistakes never live in the past

A wedding poem
friends and soul mates, husband and wife
honouring love throughout your life

terms of endearment softly spoken
vows recited, endorsed and chosen
marriage a joining shaped in the heart
encased in love till death you do part

souls entwined now the bodies have gone
together forever existing as one

Little Bird
little bird
spread your wings
take flight
leave my hand
seek your world

Condensation
hot whispers coax a pale willing canvas to life
abstract thoughts from fingers flow
fuelling the imagination
sated briefly in images of fleeting creativity
a small smile of interest escapes

a slip, a mistake
masterpieces die in simplistic motion
hot breath erasers wash across the error

hope rises for the birth of a new canvas
soft rivulets slide, hot and cold no longer in synch
art dies, masked in trails of condensation

Butterfly
neath' wings unfurled
brief life begins
a vibrant transitory journey
slowly growing into the promise of adulthood

you glide on undulating currents
beautiful, majestic, regal
dancing on shimmering heat hazes

with each rising sun, time trickles by
a slip of wing
ageing membrane betrays your fragility
weariness beckons death in fading rays.
sunset falls, wings burn
dying pirouettes twirl on a matured season

Goodbyes are hard
silence pierced
sobs tearing breaths from his body

memories seeking an audience
replaying in ultra HD
his vision shrouded in shades of mist
a final goodbye falling from his lips

they believed he would soon recover
youth was on his side, just a child
closeted whispers and furtive glances their betrayal

thirty plus years have drifted by
death often called for tea
but children never really forget
the first time the tears fell

Experimental

Free verse with a rhyming quatrain to finish, just something I felt like playing around with.

You already have the recipe
freely offered sage advice
holds one unending ingredient
time is a great healer
hogwash I say

when life hurtles like a snowball
aimless, drawn to pain in blind avenues
the passage of sun and moon
healed nothing, tempered no pain
left me floundering in turbulent seas
darkness and anger carpeting my thoughts

holding me to the ransom of memory

a soft voice sliced the agony
a recipe she bartered

pages of spilt ink to wallpaper my future
incoherent ramblings crafted into art
sterile words to soothe the waters of loss

buried years have dulled the ache
blinding the blindness of pain
holding paper thoughts in adoration

surfing rapids of personal torment
my muse sings a last lament
embracing her offered favour
I became my own saviour

The symphony that is you
notes twist in ebony tones
flowing across sensual skin
idle winds tugging at luminous strands
captured in moonlight serenades

lyrical beauty kisses neck to stomach
adagio breaths cool across summer heat
taut muscles arcing into waspish heartbeats

chords whisper to the beat of life
scales explode at the gait of thigh and calf
carrying arias in tempoed walks

a symphony of beauty, my collection
sang to the silent words of perfection
musical tones encasing you

my love, my life, all that I do

How ye Feeling
3 little words, comic sans ms
font size 10, in a blackberry hue

I pause
pondering, I seek what answer you want
truth or lie

time slips by, happy in its unhurried existence
I hesitate, vibrations ripple
their minute pulses, reminders
awoken, waiting for an answer

fingers blurring, I snake out a reply
I am fine, neither truth nor lie
3 for 3, glibness with a smile
what you wanted with deception and guile

Waiting for night
under drained smiles
I pray for night
neath' starlit skies
I douse the light

body slumping in muttered expletives
my bed sings a lullaby
a waning spirit cajoled into oblivion

Sharp Edges
behind ruby lips,
the sadism of your love breathes
stalking behind painted false smiles

like a knife, words cut deep
sliding unseen between the ribs

ghosting through flesh seeking their prize

each barbed retort,
every utterance
sharp edges tearing my exposed psyche

cruelty, your stock in trade
mind broke with each tirade
internal scars of verbal rape
bruised reminders of my escape

Puppet of time
snared in strings
tendrils of life, controlled
dancing to an unseeen tune
life's mannequin pirouhettes in grey

aches count seconds
slicing through mintues
feeding sn hourly report

destiny pulls a tightened string
sparks fly from within
ingniting defiance across the fates
freewill a myth in aging shades

Winter came back
hope ignited
first rays offer warmth
spring fell upon a starved land
first shoots rose seeking the sun
recoiling neath' frigid drops

winter-fatigued eyes
marvel at, yet hate
the trickling unique flakes
dusting their feet

Winter smiles, his job not done
smirks of snow hide the sun
extended hibernation neath' pastel slates
burning to white all he hates

An English summer day

cool breezes shuffle through the trees
stirring protesting leaves into life
swaying baskets of pinks, yellows and blues
lone colours on a drab English day

paled under slate-grey skies
colours darken, flowers shrink
memories of baked months all that remain

weather overcast, forever the same
puddles dapple every pavement
soaked reminders of the missing sun

dampness lies within the air
currents charged, lightning glare
rumbles echo around the sky
fading colours run and die

Dead town

standing proud
two supermarkets face each other
battle lines drawn
war machines in full swing

drifting down the pavement
new gaudy monoliths
imprison the foolhardy and their wages
beginning the age of the bookie

neglect follows life
two and eight lies forlorn
empty, lost, frozen in time
shop fronts caked in free advertising
their bands of commerce destroyed
in the blind stupidity of the landowners

green - amber - red,
a small posse of die-hards pause
the will to traverse the street halted
emblazoned cameos of the charity world
sparsely lit, wink beckoning messages
hand me downs twirl on manual rails
bargain hunters sucked deeper into their treasure troves

life dwindles on and their faces fade
necrotic fears seek a new parade
sunset falls, the time is late
home and future left to fate

<u>Shadow guardian</u>
shadows wait
sunset burns low
rich in the colours they hate

salivating on realisation
excitement becomes a tangible embrace
black silken armies watch the sun's final defiance
ready for their darkest of nights
fear his sword, the unknown his armour
longships, darkened sails unfolded, edge forward
copper blood ebbs into his glass

warnings scream
warmed breezes shuffle
her lullaby whispers in sensual tones

army frozen, their time elapsed
dusk filled arias, duty surpassed
an army of night slain in silent elation
sunset songs, their assassination

Tomorrow
tomorrow
false hopes, soothing questions
not now a tired lie
daily truths built on thinly-veiled promises

morning arrives
tomorrows fail to appear
yesterday tattooed on today

hope rises in the solemnity of lies
rekindling dreams in offhand smiles
maybe tomorrow a placebo for peace
buying silence till inquiries cease

The cat
paw by paw stalking
mini hunter on the prowl

stare unnerving
closer you drift
head sliding under my outstretched hand
rhythmic purrs of contentment
payment for my compliance

pristine fur rising
purr frozen
some faint sound, an early alarm call
unbetrayed by movement your claws appear
brought to life under rising hackles
before the fist bark echoes
you are gone

leaping post to post
6 feet - 9 feet - 12 feet,
always just out of reach
with feline distaste, you smirk
canine nemesis belittled

mocking smiles neath' eyes of green
goodbye imprints from a tabby queen
allowing us to feed and care for you
further control of your human zoo